Nurturing Stud

MW01014406

Nurturing Students' Character is an easy-to-use guide to incorporating social-emotional and character development (SECD) into your teaching practice. The links are clear—elementary and middle school students have better odds of academic success if you nurture their social and emotional skills. Drawing on broad field experience and the latest research, this book offers intuitive techniques for infusing your everyday teaching and classroom management with SECD opportunities. With topics ranging from self-regulation and problem solving to peer communication and empathy, these concrete strategies, practical worksheets, and self-reflective activities will help you foster a positive classroom culture.

Jeffrey S. Kress, PhD, is Dr. Bernard Heller Professor of Jewish Education at the William Davidson Graduate School of Jewish Education, Jewish Theological Seminary, USA.

Maurice J. Elias, PhD, is Professor of Psychology, Director of the Social-Emotional and Character Development Lab, and Co-Director of the Academy for Social-Emotional Learning in Schools at Rutgers University, USA. He is also a founding member of SEL4US, a national alliance of state social-emotional learning advocacy and implementation support organizations.

Nurturing Students' Character

Everyday Teaching Activities for Social-Emotional Learning

Jeffrey S. Kress and
Maurice J. Elias

Routledge
Taylor & Francis Group

NEW YORK AND LONDON

First published 2020
by Routledge
52 Vanderbilt Avenue, New York, NY 10017

and by Routledge
2 Park Square, Milton Park, Abingdon, Oxon, OX14 4RN

Routledge is an imprint of the Taylor & Francis Group, an informa business

Library of Congress Cataloging-in-Publication Data
A catalog record for this title has been requested

ISBN: 9780367190163 (hbk)
ISBN: 9780367190194 (pbk)
ISBN: 9780429199875 (ebk)

Typeset in Sabon
by Newgen Publishing UK

This book and the way our careers have developed have been greatly influenced by the wisdom and *neshama* [soul] of our late colleague and mentor, Dr. Bernard Novick. An expert in systems change, he was fond of saying that the system is perfectly designed to create the outcomes it creates. That message—to get the changes we want, we have to change our system of teaching, organizing classrooms and schools, etc.—is one we wish to acknowledge with much gratitude to Bernie. We also wish to acknowledge with deep appreciation the tremendous support given to us by our families, colleagues, students, and friends over many years. The insights in this book are as much theirs as ours.

Contents

Meet the Authors   viii

1 Introduction   1

2 A Skills-Oriented Approach to Social, Emotional, and
  Character Development   8

3 Building a Class Climate That Supports SECD   19

4 Self- and Social Awareness   33

5 Empathy and Perspective Taking   54

6 Self-Regulation   68

7 Communication and Relationship Skills   87

8 Social Problem Solving   110

9 Cross-Content SECD Elements   130

10 The Road to Success on the Journey Ahead: Using Feedback
   and Outreach to Cultivate Support and Build Expertise   155

   References   172
   Index   178

Meet the Authors

Jeffrey S. Kress, PhD, is Dr. Bernard Heller Professor of Jewish Education at the William Davidson Graduate School of Jewish Education at the Jewish Theological Seminary, USA. Dr. Kress is interested in the intersection of the social, emotional, and academic elements of education, and how these can come together to promote learning and positive character and identity development. He has written about applications of these elements not only to schools but also to informal settings such as summer camps. He is also involved in research and professional development on inclusion of learners with disabilities in a variety of educational settings.

His book, *Development, Learning, and Community: Educating for Identity in Pluralistic Jewish High Schools* (2012), won a National Jewish Book Award. In addition, he is the editor of a volume titled *Growing Jewish Minds, Growing Jewish Souls: Promoting Spiritual, Social, and Emotional Growth in Jewish Education* (2013) and co-editor of *Toward a Learning Agenda in Jewish Education* (2018). Dr. Kress is the co-author, with Bernard Novick and Maurice Elias, of *Building Learning Communities with Character: How to Integrate Academic, Social, and Emotional Learning* (2002).

Dr. Kress has also worked as a Program Development Specialist for the Social Decision Making/Social Problem Solving program of University Behavioral Health Care at Rutgers University, USA. He holds a doctorate in clinical psychology from Rutgers University.

Maurice J. Elias, PhD, is Professor and former Director of Clinical PhD Training in the Psychology Department, Director of the Rutgers Social-Emotional and Character Development Lab, and Co-Director of the Collaborative Center for Community-Based Research and Service at Rutgers University, USA. He is Co-Director of the Academy for Social and Emotional Learning in Schools and Founding Member of the Leadership Team for the Collaborative for Academic, Social, and Emotional Learning.

Dr. Elias lectures nationally and internationally, is frequently sought out as an expert in print and electronic media, and devotes his research and writing to the area of social-emotional and character development in children, schools, and families. His previous books include *The Educator's Guide to Emotional Intelligence and Academic Achievement: Social-Emotional Learning in the Classroom* (2006), *Bullying, Victimization, and Peer Harassment: A Handbook of Prevention and Intervention* (Taylor & Francis, 2007), *Urban Dreams: Stories of Hope, Character, and Resilience* (2008), *School Climate: Building Safe, Supportive and Engaging Classrooms and Schools* (2011), *Social Decision Making/Social Problem Solving Curricula for Elementary and Middle School Students* (2012), and *The Other Side of the Report Card: Assessing Students' Social, Emotional, and Character Development* (2016). He collaborated with storytellers in the U.S. and Israel and a prominent Israeli school psychologist to create a book for young children: *Talking Treasure: Stories to Help Build Emotional Intelligence and Resilience in Young Children* (2012). Most recently, he is the co-author of *The Joys and Oys of Parenting: Insights and Wisdom from the Jewish Tradition* (2016) and *Boost Emotional Intelligence in Students: 30 Flexible Research-Based Lessons to Build EQ Skills* (2018).

Dr. Elias has received the SCRA Distinguished Contribution to Practice and Ethnic Minority Mentoring Awards, APA's National Psychological Consultants to Management Award, the Joseph E. Zins Memorial Senior Scholar Award for Social-Emotional Learning from the Collaborative for Academic, Social, and Emotional Learning, the John P. McGovern Medal from the American School Health Association, and the Sanford McDonnell Award for Lifetime Achievement in Character Education. He is a licensed psychologist in New Jersey and writes a blog on Social-Emotional and Character Development for the George Lucas Educational Foundation at Edutopia.org.

Chapter 1

Introduction

What textbook will I use for science? I don't think the science textbook the school uses does a good job explaining some of the topics ... what supplemental resources will I use, and how often will I use them?

What tone do I set at the start of my class? Do I really not smile until Thanksgiving?

What do I wear on the day my principal is observing my class?

A teacher's day is full of choices. Sometimes these choices are empowering, allowing a teacher to shape her work as she desires. Some choices, however, can have the opposite effect. The classic "approach-approach conflict," for example, leaves us with a sense that in deciding among two worthy options we are forced to give up something we really want. *This ice cream tastes great ... but maybe I should have ordered the chocolate cake.* In these situations, we are occasionally pleasantly surprised to hear that we are actually facing a false choice; what we saw as an *either-or* situation is really "both-and." *Chocolate cake with a scoop of ice cream on top, anyone!?!?*

In our decades working in schools of all types, we have met many educators who share their concerns about a choice much weightier than that of ice-cream flavors: *Given the limits of time and resources, should I focus on addressing academic content or on boosting students' social, emotional, and character development (SECD)?* These educators recognize the need to scaffold students' growth in the intra- and inter-personal realms and acknowledge the impact they can have on how students interact with others, understand and manage their emotional experiences, solve problems and make healthy decisions that contribute to a caring community. At the same time, a persistent question inhibits their full engagement with this element of their work: Will I need to choose between focusing on academics and addressing issues of caring, community and character? And often, given this choice, educators choose academics.

We are not critiquing that choice—we know that there is a lot riding on academic achievement, for students and teachers alike.

Our solution does not involve cloning educators so they can get more done at once (though there are times that we would appreciate this ourselves!). Rather, existing curriculum content, instructional methods, and classroom management approaches provide ample opportunity for promoting social, emotional, and character growth. So, "yes" to doing two things simultaneously, but "no" to cloning (sorry!).

- The literature students read contains rich descriptions of relationships.
- The sentences and stories students write include descriptions of emotional states.
- The experimentation done in science involves planning and problem solving.
- The group work students do in math class requires collaboration and communication.
- The historical events students learn about involve conflicts and their consequences affecting many individuals and groups of people.

Educators have the raw material they need to simultaneously address academic content and SECD. Success, however, depends on shaping these materials into a cohesive whole—being proactive and persistent in using curricular content and instructional and class management approaches to promote positive development. Not only is this a matter of efficiency, it also is consistent with best practice in promoting social, emotional, and character growth. This book describes field-tested, teacher-and-school-validated approaches to creating classrooms and schools in which there is no need to choose between academics and SECD.

An Evolving Idea

We use the term SECD broadly, to encompass an array of approaches or movements, such as Social-Emotional Learning (SEL), character and moral education, whole child education, and positive youth development, as well as more targeted approaches like bully/violence prevention and conflict resolution. These approaches, and others, embrace the notion of education as a vehicle for growth in our relationships with others, how we understand and manage our emotions, and how we express our emotions to others. Since the time of Plato, and certainly encompassing Dewey, education has been viewed as influencing the kind of person one will become, not simply what one knows. Both Plato and Dewey emphasized the concept of education for citizenship and learning virtues, "the good," and other attitudes that "may be and often is much more important than the spelling lesson or lesson in geography or history that is learned" (Dewey, 1938, p. 48).

James Comer (1980) pioneered a developmental and psychosocial perspective to thinking about students and learning, incorporating how school and community context also served as powerful influences. Comer's School Development Project was a catalyst for many current approaches, spurred on by positive outcomes demonstrated. Daniel Goleman's (1995) international best-selling *Emotional Intelligence* provided a strong impetus for this work, with the founding of CASEL (Collaborative for Academic, Social, and Emotional Learning, www.CASEL.org) and the Character Education Partnership (www.character.org), representing the two main approaches to fostering inter- and intra-personal development in schools, following closely thereafter ("Social and Emotional Learning: A short history," 2011).

SEL's particular evolution can be traced from a social learning and cognitive-behavioral orientation (Elias, Kranzler, Parker, Kash, & Weissberg, 2014), focusing on developing skills (e.g., self-awareness, social-awareness, self-management, relationship skills, and responsible decision making). Character education emphasized the development of values or building a supportive school climate. Now, an "inexorable and long overdue" (Elias et al., 2014, p. 250) convergence of these two approaches is taking shape as an "SEL 2.0," sometimes also referred to as Social-Emotional and Character Development (SECD). Social and emotional skills "as a set of basic interpersonal competencies, can be used for good or ill; but to be used for good, they must be mastered well—Responsibility, Respect, Honesty, and other desirable aspects of character all require sound [social and emotional learning] competencies" (Elias et al., 2014, p. 261). Recommended practices associated with these two approaches also are converging (Novick, Kress, & Elias, 2002).

Noteworthy is the support of current neuroscience research about the centrality and inextricable connections of emotions and cognition. Neuroimaging of meditative practice (e.g., Lutz, Slagter, Dunne, & Davidson, 2008) fueled the popularity of mindfulness, an approach that is clearly identified as a social and emotional learning practice (Jennings, 2015).

The neurology of SECD is understood as deeply connected to the social context of development—particularly in terms of poverty and adverse childhood experiences (ACEs) being increasingly recognized for their implications for SECD. In a longitudinal study, poverty, home disorganization, and violence in the home were each found to contribute to decreased ability to regulate negative emotions in young children (Raver, Blair, & Garrett-Peters, 2015). This is of particular concern given the prevalence of ACEs—estimated at over half of students having experienced 1 ACE and 19% experiencing 3 or more (Balistreri & Alvira-Hammond, 2016)—and the number of youth living in poverty in the United States—estimated as between 21% and 43% by the National Center for Child Poverty. Racial, economic, and housing policies—the "ghosts" of which echo to this day (Lamy, 2013, p. 12)—leave issues of race and poverty deeply intertwined. Schools in high-poverty areas face high teacher turnover rates due to challenging working conditions (such as the degree of administrative support received).

> Poverty is not an acute condition, but a seemingly endless series of hurdles. These hurdles can and have been overcome, but many students also grow weary of leaping through these hurdles and drop out of the race before the end. The energy spent on leaping prevents many students from getting as far as those who need only run.
>
> (Elias, Zins, & Graczyk, 2003, p. 308)

Our approach does not mitigate the need to fight for the societal changes needed to address structural hurdles such as poverty and racism. Rather, we recognize the need to provide immediate and vital support for all students—both the hurdlers and the runners.

Is This the Parents' Role?

Why schools? Isn't it the job of the parents to instill these sorts of values and behaviors? We frequently hear this question, generally from exasperated teachers who believe that they need to make yet another choice about how to allocate their already scarce instructional time. The question reflects the assumed bifurcation of, and false choice between, the academic and social-emotional realms and the assumption that attending to the social and emotional needs of students detracts and distracts from the main work of schools—teaching subject matter.

We certainly agree that parents should take responsibility for the social and emotional development of their children. And, in the vast majority of cases, they do. It would be mistake, however, to assign parents sole responsibility, in the same way that it would be a mistake to put the onus entirely on teachers and schools. In the best cases, positive development is supported by an array of institutions—families, schools, community centers, faith-based organizations. This powerful developmental network can set norms for behavior that may not be readily evident in the glimpses of the wider world available to youth. A positive developmental network can promote self-awareness rather than self-doubt; dialogue, not defensiveness, around differences; valuing meaning and purpose, and not the pursuit of an all-but-unattainable level of celebrity and wealth.

But still, the question lingers: *Why schools? Don't schools—and especially teachers—have enough responsibilities and tasks to deal with?* Yes. However, within the parameters of the school day and school year as currently conceptualized, time can be used in different ways. School is a major ecological context in the life of youth; time spent with a teacher may eclipse that spent with a parent. Schools are social contexts for students, bringing them into contact with a diverse community of peers, teachers, and staff.

Students face emotional situations related to friendships, grades, and time management. Social and emotional issues are facts of everyday school life that interact strongly with academics, as we'll see in the next chapter. The question is not whether educators should address these issues, but rather whether they will address them proactively or reactively. Will schools function as a laboratory for living in community, or will they attempt to regulate behavior and seek to suppress social and emotional responses to reduce infractions (Osher, Kendziora, Spier, & Garibaldi, 2014).

Taking into account what Urie Bronfenbrenner would have referred to as the *ecological context of the development of SECD in schools* involves considering the multiple organizational levels that impact the experience of the child. These include the elements of the school in which the student is a direct participant, such as interactions with peers and teachers, as well as those with an indirect impact, such as the nature of staff meetings and professional development, as well as district and state/regional and national considerations.

Thinking comprehensively about a caring community supportive of SECD calls for consideration of multiple ecological elements. In our experience, this is another claim about which there is broad agreement among educators and, at the same time, consternation. There is no denying the complexity of the system in which youth are embedded; the social, emotional and character development of our students has a wide array of influences which may complement and augment the work of educators or which may stand in opposition. What are my efforts worth, a teacher may wonder, when student behavior is so strongly shaped by the chaos of the Internet, when screaming is the new discussing, and when discerning the truth and the perspective of sources can be challenging? We are sympathetic to this concern and recognize that teachers can't be the only answer. However, we are also moved by the Talmudic maxim: "You are not required to complete the task, nor are you free to desist from it." Let's not underestimate the power of educators and schools!

Of course, at the same time that teachers are "not desisting" from promoting SECD, they must also not desist from addressing academic outcomes. This persistent pursuit of growth of the whole student—social, emotional, character *and* academic—is our focus. Teachers should not need to choose which among these is most important—they are interdependent.

Education Through an SECD Lens

Photographers use filtered lenses to accentuate some colors while deemphasizing others. The complex hues of the subject still exist; the photographer chooses to look at some and not others. What would education look like if viewed through a SECD lens? Such a lens would allow us to look at the social and emotional elements already present in an ordinary classroom. We would see these social and emotional elements most clearly through the **content** of what is taught; the **pedagogy** used to teach it; and the class (and school) **context** in which the teaching takes place.

Content. The cliché about schools focusing on "facts and figures" does not describe the sort of learning called for by contemporary curriculum standards. Learning *about* a topic area is not sufficient; educators are called upon to help students *learn how to think about* a topic. The analysis done by UCLA's National Center for History in the Schools' Historical Thinking Standards, which align with Common Core Standards, provides a telling case in point. Far from being the dry memorization of facts and figures that some of us might remember from our own social studies classes, history should be presented in a way that emphasizes the emotions and decisions of people facing particular circumstances, their "motives, beliefs, interests, hopes, and fears,"[1] the consequences of their decisions, and the possible outcomes of decisions not taken. Social studies shifts from being a study of historical events to being a study of people in context. Not only is such an approach likely to motivate students but it also opens the door for applying social studies to understanding one's *own* life in context. Our lens will focus on manifestations of SECD throughout the curriculum, from understanding characters' emotions in literature to problem solving in math and science.

Pedagogy. Many administrators have told us they get concerned when they consistently hear silence while walking by a classroom. Though a teacher might welcome quiet moments—and we recognize the importance of infusing class time with occasional quiet moments—the administrators' concerns come from a fundamental belief in pedagogy as a social process. Our SECD lens would reveal that it is frequently a *noisy* social process! By hearing their peers' interpretations of a text or event, students sharpen their own ideas. Working in groups, students learn new ways of solving problems. Feedback from a peer on one's work may be treated with at least as much gravity as that from teachers. These pedagogical techniques are not new, nor are they somehow negated by the introduction of educational technology. In using social pedagogies, teachers often attend to elements of SECD, generally when these break down. Keeping paired assignments, group work, and class discussions on track requires attention to their social and emotional dimensions. Our approach asks that teachers do this proactively and intentionally.

Context. *Each morning, students enter the classroom having politely greeted you at the door to the room. They are well-rested, well-fed, centered, and focused on learning. They have set aside all of life's anxiety and any emotional baggage they may have with one another and with you. They've come to learn ... and only to learn!* If this describes your class on a regular basis, you are in a very small minority. The rest of us can appreciate that no matter the content or pedagogy, instructional activities are just one piece of the social and emotional life of classrooms. The SECD lens reveals many contextual factors connected to learning: Is the environment stimulating? Distracting? Are relationships in the class marked by friendships? Animosities? Frenemyships? Do students experience the classroom as a safe place or do they perceive antagonism from peers or from the teacher? Do they come to class exhausted? Hungry? Angry?

Stressed? The often-used term *ready to learn* refers to much more than whether students remembered to bring in their pencils and notebooks. In fact, teachers often tell us that they spend as much or more time on classroom management as they do on instruction. The classroom context, or climate, sets the stage for student learning. Classroom management can be done in a way that both facilitates learning and enhances SECD.

SECD and Academics

This book provides suggestions for how teaching academic content areas can be coupled with enhancing SECD. It is worth noting that improvements in SECD can have an impact on the learning that goes on in a classroom. In their review of the topic, Zins and colleagues (2004, p. 14) conclude that an array of "studies found a broad range of outcomes related to school success that resulted from SEL interventions." When there is attention given to building positive social and emotional dynamics in a classroom, students are able to support one another, they feel safe taking risks and expressing themselves, can manage the emotional ups and downs of the school day, and are able to focus on learning. Long (2019, p. 1) points to "a virtuous cycle in which effective SEL implementation reduces time spent on classroom management and allows more time for teaching and learning." Teaching cannot proceed effectively, and learning cannot be internalized and generalized, in classroom environments that are not managed as caring, supportive, safe, challenging communities of learners.

Organization of This Book

The following two chapters describe components that form the foundation for all SECD-enhancing efforts. Chapter 2 introduces a skill-building framework to social and emotional competencies, highlighting the need to address behaviors, knowledge, and emotions in concert with one another. In Chapter 3, we provide suggestions for creating a caring classroom learning community. Individual SECD competency areas are introduced in Chapters 4 through 8, with strategies and examples included for each. The final two chapters widen the focus. In Chapter 9, we connect SECD promotion to education that takes place beyond individual content areas. This chapter discusses behavior management, SECD-enhancing pedagogies, and student motivation. Finally, Chapter 10 provides information about how to take the first steps in your SECD journey, and how to assess your progress.

Note

1 https://phi.history.ucla.edu/nchs/alignment-common-core-standards/3-historical-analysis-interpretation/ (accessed 16 October, 2019).

Chapter 2

A Skills-Oriented Approach to Social, Emotional, and Character Development

Our SECD lens reveals the deep connection of academic, social, and emotional learning infused throughout a school. A comprehensive approach to promoting SECD would be similarly multifaceted. A web search of *social and emotional learning* or of *character education* will yield a lifetime's worth of "hits." One would quickly realize that there is no shortage of books, curricula, and providers of professional development in these areas. While we applaud this blossoming of the field, we are also concerned about the potential misleading messages that social and emotional growth can be addressed by using only a few activities or techniques, or that these activities or techniques should exist on a plane parallel to that of academics. It is tempting to take a checklist approach to promoting SECD:

> Assembly about bullying? Check!
> Signs in the halls highlighting our values? Check!
> A few minutes each week dedicated to an SECD curriculum? Check!
> Doing SECD for one entire marking period? Check!

These elements of an SECD approach are common; we don't mean to imply that they have no place in a school. We see them, however, as parts of a much larger whole that must address the complexity of how social-emotional competencies and character develop. Because efforts to address SECD in schools, ideally, happen on multiple levels (individual, class, grade-level); involve multiple constituents (teachers, administrators, paraprofessionals); and consist of multiple methodologies, deciding where to start describing this system is likely to result in oversimplification. A teacher's SECD journey needs to start somewhere, and we've found it helpful to start with the notion of skill building.

A Grounding in Skills

Think of the social and emotional skills called upon over the course of a day, or even over the course of a single interaction: A teacher sees a student sitting alone on the floor in the hall. What might that student be feeling; what non-verbal clues exist as to why the student is sitting alone in the hall? Have we seen anything like that in the past? What is supposed to be happening for the student now—where should that student be? What is the teacher's initial emotional reaction to seeing the student? Might the teacher need to regulate her emotions as the situation unfolds, with initial anger over a student being out of class evolving into empathy once the student's emotional state is clear? What tone of voice and what phrasing would the teacher use when speaking with the student? How will this be modulated as the conversation unfolds? What will the teacher decide to say to his student? Regardless, it will have an impact on the emotional state of that student and will likely involve other people. Send the child back to class? Engage in a conversation about what's going on? Bring the student to a counselor or administrator's office? Contact parents/guardians?

Handling a situation like this—one example of many similar ones facing educators every day—requires many skills. What are they? We've found the rubric provided by CASEL (casel.org) to be helpful in organizing what could become an unwieldly list. CASEL uses five broad categories:

1. Self-awareness (e.g., identifying one's emotional state).
2. Self-regulation (e.g., the ability to calm oneself during times of stress).
3. Social awareness (e.g., empathy or perspective taking).
4. Relationship skills (e.g., communication and listening skills).
5. Problem solving and decision-making skills (e.g., the ability to anticipate consequences of one's choices).

Thinking about SECD as rooted in skills leads us to seek ways to build these skills and not just have students *learn about* them. Because these skills are relevant at every age level, and during every school day, we need to have comprehensive ways of building them over time—just like we do for reading and math skills.

But what does it take to build a skill? The answer to this question does not need to emerge from an esoteric psycho-educational theory. Rather, we all have skills and abilities that we've developed over time. We are not referring to skills that might be considered unprecedented or superhuman. Yes, some readers may have mastered the skills involved in high-altitude mountaineering or piloting spacecraft. For the rest of us:

> Think of something that you've learned how to do that not everyone knows how to do, but that many others know how to do.

Do you play a musical instrument? Paint? Play tennis? Do you know a card trick? Can you write a lesson plan or develop a curricular unit?

OK, now think of what was involved in going from *not able to do this* to *being able to do this.*

Chances are you didn't come into the world with this particular ability. Developing it might have come easily ... or not. We've found this to be a prompt that is both generative and fun when done with groups of educators. Once everyone has thought of a skill or talent, they can compare notes in pairs or small groups, with each member sharing their talent and, importantly, enumerating the steps taken to acquire the talent. The excitement over sharing one's talent and learning about the often heretofore unknown talents of peers is just a prelude to the core discussion around how these talents were acquired. In that discussion, similarities become clear and differences tend to be matters of emphasis rather than substance.

At the most basic level, there is the identification of a domain. *I'm good at ... or I know how to ...* The specificity of the domain varies. Cooking. Cooking Indian food. Cooking vegetarian Indian food. Cooking Samosas. Playing soccer or being a soccer goalie. Regardless, there is some shorthand that conveys what one is talking about and provides *some*—but not detailed—guidance to those we speak with. It says, "I know what vegetarian cooking is about even if I can't do it." We need a name for what we're talking about. In our case, establishing a SECD vocabulary that can be used as shorthand for prompts and cues is a basic step in the skill-building process.

In naming our competencies, we usually do not start on a very micro level ("I am good at moving the spatula in a swirling motion while stir-frying eggplant in peanut oil"). We start with a broader domain ("I'm a good cook"). Acquiring competence in a domain, though, involves the cumulative development of micro-level skills. One may set out to become a better cook, and that goal can provide a motivating vision of one's goal as well as a shorthand for what someone is doing, but in order to actually grow within the broad domain, one needs to dig deeper to get to a level of skills. What does a good cook need to know? To be able to do? Can I tell kale from Swiss chard? Can I braise, broil, bake, and brine?

The development of component ("micro") skills may not be glamorous, but it is foundational. How does it happen? While there is no singular process, there are elements that recur in the stories we hear. Box 2.1 summarizes the instructional process leading to skill development. Below, we comment on some of the most salient elements.

First, most practical abilities are rarely developed in isolation; we tend to draw on existing wisdom as input. At the very least, we use a guide book or an instructional video. Often, we benefit from more active involvement of others with more experience: an instructor, teacher, coach, advisor, or mentor. But what does this person do?

Modeling, With Intentional Instruction

There is perhaps no charge to an educator more frequently heard than "Be a good role model!" Watching an expert—or at least someone with more competence—leads to a mental picture, or schema, of what the skills look like in action. One can read a description of how to plant one's feet prior to taking a jump shot in basketball, but that's a poor substitute for seeing someone doing it. To this, we add a dimension of *intentionality*. Why? If a coach is modeling, wouldn't it, by definition, be intentional? Perhaps in a literal sense (that is, the coach is not modeling *accidentally*), but not in terms of maximal modeling. When a good coach sets out to model a skill, she would do it differently than she would if enacting the skill herself in an applied situation. The coach would likely do one or more of these:

- slow down the action;
- over-emphasize certain elements to make them more apparent to the novice;
- narrate the process ("Now I'm going to put my right foot down while pivoting on my left foot"); and
- pause artificially to highlight a particular moment ("Look at where my toes are pointed once I put my right foot down").

In short, there is more to successful modeling than a novice watching an expert "in action."

Practice With Feedback

Wouldn't it be nice to go directly from "see it done" to "be able to do it well?" As we all know, though, the hard work of practice is needed. The importance of practice has propelled itself further into common consciousness through the idea, generally attributed to Malcom Gladwell, that 10,000 hours of practice are needed to achieve expertise. The frequent misapplication of the "10,000 hours" rule has spawned a vigorous backlash, including from Gladwell himself.[1] *How* one practices is at least as important as *how long* one practices.

Practice needs to be more than "try and try again." Feedback needs to be given and incorporated so that each "hour" of practice can represent improvement and not simply repetition. It is often the case that some degree of feedback is provided by the activity itself. The stir-fry comes out bland. The jump shot goes wide to the right. And, sometimes, the learner has enough information from this natural feedback and/or from prior experience to self-correct. Add more salt, garlic, and hot sauce to the stir fry. Aim the ball farther to the left. In many cases, however, this is inadequate. First, a high degree of self-monitoring may be needed, and this self-monitoring could, until the skill becomes more automatic, distract from the practice itself. Without an outside observer providing input, I may pay so much attention to the placement of my right foot, that I neglect the rest of the shot. Or, I may think that I am pointing my toes in the right direction, when in reality I'm a bit off target. Second, the novice may need additional tips or information that would be hard to come by through trial and error. I might stumble upon the way to thicken my stir-fry sauce, but it would take an awful lot of trial and error. Some situations have particularly high stakes—learning to drive a car by trial and error, rather than by expert coaching, can lead to serious injury, or at least high insurance payments!

Generalization to Increasing Complexity

Complex skills are best taught step-wise, focusing on component parts. As an undergraduate, one of the authors took an extracurricular fencing course. He knew it would not involve swashbuckling Hollywood-style sword fights but was still surprised when an entire session was devoted to various ways to grip one's weapon, and the proper way to transition from one grip to another. After practicing this and other subsequently learned pieces, the novice fencers started linking these together into more complex actions which actually started to feel like fencing (though it may have looked more like a group of awkward bee-keepers in ill-fitting outfits).

The Yerkes-Dodson principle is a well-documented guideline—the degree of challenge should be appropriate for the skill. The best time for "Let's learn how to dribble the basketball with our non-dominant hands" is not during a competitive game, though eventually a competition will be an excellent practice opportunity. A good coach works up to this—practice in drills, use during practice scrimmages, and then use in a game—and not in a close game, at least initially.

The analogy of learning to drive a car points to another important element of skill building, namely the increasing complexity of the context in which learning takes place. In most cases (though there is inevitably someone at each workshop who is an exception!), we don't learn to drive on a crowded highway. We learn when the stakes are lower and gradually work our way up. Being able to enact a skill in a calm, ideal situation doesn't automatically transfer to being able to do it when the chips are down.

Role plays provide excellent opportunities to practice skills and form the basis of several of the activities in this book. Role plays engage students physically, as well as socially and emotionally. They allow more exuberant students a chance to exuberate and provide more socially tentative students with scaffolding for participation. Further, as Robert Selman, a leading SECD researcher, puts it, such activities can "lead participants away from their own egocentric reactions" in a way that is an "immediate rather than an intellectual experience" (Selman, 2003, p. 70).

> [T]he student who is asked to play a particular role must directly engage that character's attitudes, assumptions, and emotions—in other words, move away from his or her own point of view to stand for a while in another person's shoes.
>
> (Selman, 2003, p. 70)

Motivation

When we draw an analogy between developing SEL skills and developing other skills, the issue of motivation inevitably emerges. We learned our skills (cooking, sports) because we wanted to, because we saw it as intrinsically motivating ("it is fun, satisfying") and/or extrinsically so ("I'll impress my friends", "I can see my art online"). What's the motivation for developing SEL skills? There is no singular response to this. Sometimes, students will see (or can come to see) tangible, short-term, benefits in their lives ("I won't get in trouble so often" or "I'll be more effective in expressing myself"). Sometimes, they will respond to an appeal to virtues, or becoming the type of person they want to become. Others will relate to the benefits of a safe and caring community and the need for SEL skills in maintaining it. A skilled coach seeks to understand the motivations of individual team members and helps novices keep their larger goals in mind even when focusing on tasks that may seem only distantly related.

Reflect Regularly

As Dewey (1938) put it, we don't learn from experience, we learn from reflecting on experience. Noted developmental psychologist Irving Sigel pointed out that in order for our ideas, beliefs, or schemas (Sigel would use the term "representational competence") to evolve, we need to become aware of how these are supported by, or in conflict with, new experiences (Sigel, 1993; Sigel & Kelly, 1988). To achieve this, we need "distance" from our currently-held schemas; to Sigel, the job of the educator is to set the stage for this distancing and to encourage learners to reflect on the ramifications of their experiences.

To borrow a term from another noted developmental psychologist, David Elkind (1988), children's lives are often "hurried." And, if this was true about youth in 1988 when Elkind wrote about them, it is all the more true now. And it is not only students who have hurried (or harried!) lives— so do adults. Multitasking is for many people a way of life, despite occasional reminders from researchers that we tend to overestimate our ability to do so effectively. From a learning perspective, a harried existence works against learning from experience. To counter this, educators need to provide moments for reflection. This can occur through written journaling or small group discussion. Throughout this book, you'll find many opportunities to create reflective opportunities in the service of building SECD and academics.

Linking Skills and Virtues

The convergence of the SEL and Character Education movements represents a growing appreciation of the importance of linking skills and virtues (Elias et al., 2014). Skills are building blocks. What is built from these can take many forms. One can use problem-solving skills to avoid a fight, or to figure out how to avoid being caught for starting a fight. Assertive communication skills can be used to ask for help when needed, or to try to pressure a peer into a poor decision.

Box 2.1. Encouraging Students' Use of Skills

1. Naming

- Establish terminology to serve as a shorthand for the skill or set of skills.
- Example: "We're going to be practicing Keep Calm as a way to help with stress."

2. Building motivation

- Work with students to understand why these skills could be helpful in their lives.
- Example, in introducing listening skills, ask students to reflect on how it feels when a friend listens carefully to them as opposed to ignores what they say.

3. Modeling

- **Showing students how** to use ideas from the SEL lessons is more effective than **telling** students to use them.
  - Example: When introducing a theme, discuss when it is important in your own life.
    - This does not have to be discussed in any detail.
    - You can focus on your professional life, not your personal life.

4. Prompting and Cueing Concepts and Skills Learned Previously

- **Reminding students** to use skills will promote students' generalization of skills.
  - Ask, "How does what we spoke about in October's leadership theme help us with this situation?" These prompts add up over the three years that students spend in the SEL instructional context.
- Students learn that SEL lessons are good for advice and practical help.

5. Pedagogy for Generalizing Skills

- **Review**
  - Generalization of skills comes from deep learning and guided practice.
  - Review prior activities for the students who were present, those who were absent, and those who were present but not fully attentive.

- Repetition
  - Students will not learn the skills in one lesson.
  - Repetition helps students find out how to flexibly apply the skill in many circumstances.
- Reminders
  - **Anticipate:** When you know about an upcoming opportunity to use new skills, remind students in advance that it will help them to use the skill
  - **Visual Reminders:** Place (student-made, ideally) posters, signs, and reminders of SEL themes and skills in classrooms, guidance offices, group rooms, the main office, on bulletin boards.
  - **Testimonials:** Use sharing circles so students can share examples of times they have used skills (or could have used them to good advantage if they would have remembered to do so).
  - **Prompts:** Develop verbal and nonverbal prompts to remind students to use skills.
- Reinforcement
  - Students are especially attuned to appreciation, both from adults and from peers. So be alert to students "living" the SEL themes.
- Reflection
  - Build into many SEL activities.
  - Opportunities for reflection (discussion, journaling, etc.) build a habit of thoughtfulness.

Talk of "virtues," though, raises important questions: Which virtues? Is there a list? A set of priorities or weighting? Do parents share these priorities with the school? Do staff members within a school share priorities? In any morally complex situation, multiple, sometimes conflicting, virtues come into play. Context and learning history play central roles (we are all familiar with times that "honesty" must be weighed against "respect for the other person's feelings"). At best, virtues provide a set of guideposts for behavior. Students require social and emotional competence to figure out how to navigate any given situation.

How school leaders can facilitate discussion around virtues is a matter beyond the scope of this book. For classroom teachers, it is important to think about any small number of virtues that can help guide SECD efforts and to weave these into discussions of classroom expectations. To get this process started, we have summarized some approaches to the topic:

Signature Strengths Approach

The following virtues—also called "signature strengths"—were identified as being universal across all cultures and major religions. It has been suggested that human beings have an evolutionary predisposition regarding these virtues, suggesting that these behaviors have emerged and been sustained because each one solves a problem related to survival (Dahlsgaard, Peterson, & Seligman, 2005).

- Courage: Emotional strengths that involve the exercise of will to accomplish goals in the face of opposition, external or internal; examples include bravery, perseverance, and authenticity.
- Justice: Civic strengths that underlie healthy community life; examples include fairness, leadership, and citizenship or teamwork.
- Humanity: Interpersonal strengths that involve "tending and befriending" others; examples include love and kindness.
- Temperance: Strengths that protect against excess; examples include forgiveness, humility, prudence, and self-control.
- Wisdom: Cognitive strengths that entail the acquisition and use of knowledge; examples include creativity, curiosity, judgment, and perspective.
- Transcendence: Strengths that forge connections to the larger universe and thereby provide meaning; examples include gratitude, hope, and spirituality (Dahlsgaard et al., 2005, p. 205).

Mastering Our Skills and Inspiring Character (MOSAIC)

Working with low-income, disadvantaged, urban minority students, the Rutgers SECD Lab identified a set of virtues that they believe underlie motivation to master academic content as well as behavior in a socially, emotionally, and ethically competent matter. The MOSAIC approach uses a spiral curriculum model to integrate SEL and character virtue instruction over a three-year period (www.secdlab.org/MOSAIC). Note the valence added to each of the virtues—it may be useful to ask students to consider what the difference might be without the first word in each case.

1. Positive Purpose
2. Optimistic Future-Mindedness
3. Responsible Diligence
4. Helpful Generosity
5. Compassionate Forgiveness and Gratitude
6. Constructive Creativity

KIPP Schools Approach

KIPP schools are strongly identified with the words of Dr. Martin Luther King, Jr., who said "Intelligence plus character—that is the goal of true education." Accordingly, KIPP schools intentionally build character in their students as an essential complement to academic excellence, using the framework below:

1. **Zest:** Approaching life with excitement and energy; feeling alive and activated.

    Example Indicators: Actively participates; shows enthusiasm; invigorates others.

2. **Self-Control:** Regulating what one feels and does; being self-disciplined.

    Example Indicators: Comes to class prepared; pays attention and resists distractions; remains calm even when criticized or otherwise provoked; keeps temper in check.

3. **Gratitude:** Being aware of and thankful for opportunities that one has and for good things to happen.

    Example Indicators: Recognizes what others have done; shows appreciation for others; appreciates and/or shows appreciation for his/her opportunities.

4. **Curiosity:** Taking an interest in experience and learning new things for its own sake; finding things fascinating.

    Example Indicators: Is eager to explore new things; asks and answers questions to deepen understanding; actively listens to others; asks appropriate, probing questions.

5. **Optimism:** Expecting the best in the future and working to achieve it.

    Example Indicators: Gets over frustrations and setbacks quickly; believes that effort will improve his or her future; can articulate positive future aspirations and connects current actions to those aspirations.

6. **Grit:** Finishing what one starts; completing something despite obstacles; a combination of persistence and resilience.

    Example Indicators: Finishes whatever he or she begins; tries very hard even after experiencing failure; works independently with focus despite distractions.

7. **Social Intelligence:** Being aware of motives and feelings of other people and oneself; ability to reason within large and small groups.

    Example Indicators: Able to find solutions during conflicts with others; demonstrates respect for feelings of others; knows when and how to include others.

In summary, social and emotional skills need to be guided by virtues; virtues need to be enacted with skills. Because virtues are guidelines and not instructions, it is important to reflect on how we put these virtues/attributes into action in order to further hone our understanding of their nuances.

Note

1 www.nytimes.com/2018/05/29/magazine/malcolm-gladwell-likes-things-better-in-canada.html (accessed 16 October, 2019).

Chapter 3

Building a Class Climate That Supports SECD

When you go into a restaurant to have a nice meal, you want the environment to be welcoming, relaxed, calm, organized, and professional. If the food is great but the ambiance is miserable, you will be unlikely to want to return and you will be most likely to remember the tumult and not the food.

It's no different for our students coming to class. They want to be in a climate that is good for learning—welcoming, relaxed, calm, organized, professional, but also warm, supportive, and caring. If the curriculum content is great but the climate is miserable, students are not likely to be eager to come back to that classroom and they are also unlikely to remember what was being taught to them.

So it is clear that SECD, classroom climate, and learning are deeply intertwined. When members of the classroom community incorporate SECD into their behavior—demonstrating empathy, respectful communication, self-control and the like—the classroom climate improves as relationships deepen and conflict is reduced. In turn, the everyday components of classroom life provide natural opportunities for SECD growth and for learning to flourish.

As much as we might like it to be the case, the thresholds to our classrooms are not magical portals that generate enthusiasm and readiness for learning as students enter. It is not surprising to learn that

> studies report strong associations between achievement levels and classrooms that are perceived as having greater cohesion and goal-direction, and less disorganization and conflict. Research also suggests that the impact of classroom climate may be greater on students from low-income homes and groups that often are discriminated against.
>
> (Adelman & Taylor, 2005, p. 89)

A Caring Community of SECD Practice

There is a deep connection between individual and communal SECD functioning. The collective set of individual social and emotional competencies
of community members contributes to the nature of the collective—a group
with members who regularly demonstrate empathy with one another will
feel and function quite differently than a group in which many members
do not. Communal norms and expectations, in turn, shape the expression
of individual skills—a community in which empathy is regularly practiced
perpetuates this behavior among its members.

In practice, this means that we cannot address individual SECD without
also considering the nature of the community. The community provides
the fertile soil in which individuals' SECD can thrive; enacting SECD
returns nutrients to enrich the soil from which it grows. As Jackson,
Borstrom, and Hansen (1993) and others have famously pointed out,
schools have a "moral life"—the regularities and routines of a school
"teach" students what is expected of members of this community. The
environment provides cues for behaviors. When the realities of interactions in the environment run counter to the rhetoric around values and
norms—when adults in the school don't "walk their talk"—the students
are watching hypocrisy.

- Do the adults in the school speak respectfully of, and with, students?
  Other adults?
- Is the community welcoming to diverse individuals? Are those who are
  potentially at the margins afforded more than just the rhetoric of a
  safe space, and actually experience the agency and empowerment of full
  community involvement?
- What accomplishments are rewarded publicly?
- To what extent do students have the opportunity to contribute in meaningful ways to their school community? To what extent is the school
  community actively engaged in efforts to contribute to the betterment
  of those beyond the school walls?

In this chapter, we address steps teachers can take to maximize the SECD-
enhancing potential of their classrooms.

It Starts Before the Beginning

We can start building community in the classroom even before the students
enter by attending to the arrangement and appearance of the room. As
Sizer and Sizer (1999) remind us, educators are always sending messages to
students—intended or not—and the students, in turn, are watching. What
do they see when they enter the classroom? In an intentionally-designed

SECD classroom, the space itself would help students become knowledgeable, responsible, respectful, non-violent, and caring members of the class community. The walls of the classroom would support SECD efforts by being spaces to highlight student work demonstrating a range of student strengths—academic work, and also art, photography, etc. The teacher's attention to a range of learners would be evident in the posted visual aids and prompts that can be used by students who need them. While teachers may have constraints on the arrangement of their classroom furniture, configurations of desks and chairs can, to the extent possible, reflect a desire for interaction, and allow students to respond to one another face to face.

The transition into the classroom is not all about inanimate objects. Perhaps the most important tone-setting element the students encounter is the educator they meet when they enter a classroom. There is a technique that teachers can use that is powerful enough to set a tone, model communication skills, and show care and concern. Luckily, it is a fairly easy technique to master—greeting each student by name as they enter the classroom. This is more than a social nicety; it can have real behavioral impact. For example, Allday and Pakurar (2007) found that when teachers started greeting students with behavior problems at the doors of their classroom, sizable increases in on-task classroom behavior resulted. Similar findings come from extensive research from the Responsive Classroom program, which features greetings and morning meetings at the start of the day as cornerstones of its proven efforts to improve students' social-emotional and academic development (www.responsiveclassroom.org). Just as we like to be greeted warmly when we enter a home, house of worship, or business, children of all ages like to be welcomed into the classroom. A warm, personal welcome, by name, can set the tone for learning!

Transition to Learning Checklist

☐ Arrange your classroom in a way that reflects your goals for student-centered, community-oriented learning, with a seating arrangement that allows students to see one another and engage one another directly in discussion.

☐ Welcome students individually, by name, as they enter the classroom.

☐ Post student work in a way that emphasizes an array of student strengths.

☐ Let displays such as bulletin boards reflect the diversity of the student body.

☐ Use visual aids and prompts that can be seen by students who would benefit from them.

☐ Display visual reminders of the classroom constitution and/or SECD skills and principles central to the class, and refer to these often.

The checklist above is designed to reflect best practices that can be visible to anyone walking into your classroom—it is based on observables, rather than attributes that might have to be inferred.

Classroom Interactions

Community Psychologist Jim Kelly (1979) pointed out, modifying the refrain from a jazz song, that when it comes to making an impact, "'Tain't (just) what you do, it's the way that you do it." We have all experienced the mismatch of seemingly well-intentioned behavior delivered with apparent negativity, help delivered begrudgingly, or a discussion of an important concern infused with boredom. *The content of what we teach is of course crucial, but how it is delivered can make or break the SECD climate and academic learning of a class.* The non-verbal components of communication, for example, provide meta-messages that may convey more, and more accurate, information than what is actually said. Our true emotions are apt to emerge in non-verbal "slippage" despite our best efforts. For an educator, this shows the importance of authenticity; to fully act patient, for example, one must actually embrace patience in the moment. Educators must also be sensitive to students' non-verbal cues that might indicate confusion or disengagement and help students name those feelings and learn to express them appropriately.

Our responses to our students can either open or shut the door to a community of learning. Some of this is simple behavioral reinforcement—if a student feels embarrassed when offering an incorrect answer, it is unlikely she will want to participate further. An educator can respond to errors, or claims that "I don't know," in a way that normalizes such responses as part of the learning process. The way we ask questions, too, can draw students into a discussion. Open-ended questions encourage answers longer than one word. Requests for other perspectives, even when a satisfactory response is provided, can encourage divergent, creative thinking. "Wait time"—allowing the often uncomfortable silence that sometimes follows a question—can let students think before they respond, and allow participation from even those students who might process more slowly.

In a learning classroom community, students will lead and contribute along with you. Students can be encouraged to work collaboratively, to help one another, and to discuss important ideas in pairs or small groups. Students can help bring absentees up to speed, and those who finish class work more quickly can help those who need it. Collaborative work can serve as a jumping-off point for students to reflect on their interactions, illuminating strengths as well as goals for improvement. Many teachers use a format such as the "Sharing Circle" (Box 3.1) to help build classroom community.

Box 3.1. The Sharing Circle

Many readers will be familiar with some form of "circle time" or "class meeting." There are several intersections of SECD work and sharing circles, or class meetings. We'll use the term "Sharing Circle" in our discussion, while recognizing that this goes by many names (Morning Meeting; Team Huddle; etc.).

Structure. Sharing Circles can take many forms, physically. As the name suggests, a circle is the preferred format, allowing students to speak to the group and not to the back of the head of the person in front of them. If logistics allow a full class to meet as one, that's great. If not, then this can happen in smaller groups.

Think of the Sharing Circle as a ritual. It is something that is done regularly, not only "as needed." Some teachers use it as a transition ritual, marking the beginning and/or end of the day, or a return from lunch or recess.

A "Speaker Power" object (a wand or stuffed animal) can be a helpful tool in concretizing the notion that one person (the holder of the Speaker Power) speaks at a time.

It can also be helpful to establish non-verbal signals for use in Sharing Circles (and throughout the day!). For example, patting one's chest as a sign of agreement.

Function. What is shared in a Sharing Circle? What is this venue used for?

As a transition ritual, the "content" can be something as basic as asking students to greet a fellow student by name. Some educators ask students to share news about themselves or check in about how they are feeling. We've seen teachers start each session by asking each student to dedicate their learning for the day to someone or something.

The Sharing Circle can also be a space in which to be extra intentional about SECD in the classroom. It can serve as the place to discuss class norms and expectations and to reflect on how the class is doing in upholding these and on what changes may be needed. It can be a venue for introducing and practicing skills that are introduced throughout this book. As the Sharing Circle becomes a part of the class routine, it can be called on as a format for engaging in difficult conversations.

Sharing Circles are also opportunities for community building, for students to get to know one another. This can be done through posing questions that allow for students to use their imaginations while also sharing an element of themselves:

- If you could have any superpower, what would you pick and why?
- If you could be any animal for one day, what would you pick and why?

Getting to know one another can also take place in a way that is linked to content:

- If you could spend the day with one character from our book, who would you pick and why?
- If you were able to go back in time to meet and ask a question of one of the presidents we've been learning about, which president would you meet and what would you ask?
- Which invention from the Industrial Revolution do you think was most useful and why do you think so?
- Which part of the science experiment did you find most exciting and why?

In a learning community, the language of SECD is commonly heard. Teachers not only model respectful behavior, but also discuss their emotions, and ask students about theirs. Modeling SECD skills involves going beyond enacting positive behavior; it involves thinking aloud, sharing thought processes so that students can have a glimpse into otherwise invisible behavior that plays out "in one's head."

Summary: Classroom Interactions Checklist

☐ Be sensitive to the non-verbal signs that students are confused or otherwise disengaged.

☐ Explicitly model positive SECD behaviors, especially when stressed.

☐ Respond to wrong answers, or responses of "I don't know," in a way that shows that this is part of the process of learning.

☐ Use curricular materials—for example, in history, current events, literature etc.—to highlight positive communal behavior.

☐ Help students articulate their own learning and SECD goals, to foster their responsibility for sustaining a positive classroom climate and learning environment.

☐ When using group work, take time to help students process their interactions and set goals for improvement.

☐ Ask students to give, accept, and defend clear and specific feedback to one another, challenge them to explain their reasoning of things, and encourage them to engage in defining and solving problems.

☐ Use pair-shares, small group work, buddying, and in general allow students to help one another, bring absentees up to speed, etc.

☐ Have students who finish worksheets or writing tasks first help others who may be having difficulty.

☐ Use questioning strategies (such as asking open-ended questions, using "wait time," and prompting for additional responses) that can foster divergent, creative thinking, and reinforce the existence of multiple opinions.

Behavioral Expectations

As in all communities, classroom norms and expectations are sometimes violated. Infractions create critical junctures in which reactions can either promote or stifle feelings of community. It is often at these times that it is most difficult to maintain a community-enhancing stance and to model respectful, caring behavior. At a minimum, rules should be consistently enforced and positive behaviors identified and reinforced. Further, an SECD-informed approach to classroom management can help you be proactive and, when needed, react in a way that maintains relationships and builds skills. It begins with how norms are established to start with.

Establishing Norms

To adapt an old saying, an ounce of prevention is worth at least a pound of disciplinary action. Community building itself can play a role in promoting positive behavior—as students feel more connected to you, to their peers, and to the school, they will be more willing to follow the community's behavioral expectations. Many educators take the important preventive step of engaging students in the process of developing and monitoring the norms and expectations for behavior.

For example, the following prompts for a discussion about class norms are adapted from the MOSAIC curriculum (www.secdlab.org/MOSAIC):

- Explain that norms are agreements that we make for how we work together in our class community.
- Questions for discussion
  - Why is it important that we all agree on these norms?
  - How will we keep each other accountable for sticking to these norms?
  - How will we decide if we need to change these norms or add something to our list?
  - What's one norm we've already established as we've developed this set of rules? (Examples: working together, respectful listening, collaboration, etc.)
  - What are some other norms that can help us learn together as a community?
      Note: Close by commenting realistically on how the class communicated with each other and dealt with disagreements. If the process was not smooth, indicate that these are areas you will all work on and that you are sure they will learn to work better together in the coming weeks.

Many teachers formalize this process by creating a class "constitution" that sets out rules that would best allow learning to take place (see Appendix A for examples of classroom constitutions). Like any set of laws, the class constitution must be a "living document"; its prominent display in the classroom is necessary but ultimately insufficient for success. Check-ins are important; ask for reflection on how the class as a community is doing in terms of following through on their agreements. What elements, for example, have been particularly challenging to follow? What are some suggestions for being more successful at this? Are there any new agreements that should be added? Anything need to be changed? This sort of goal setting about community-oriented behaviors can be done on an individual level as well, through developing Legacy Goals (Box 3.2).

Box 3.2. Setting Legacy Goals (for Grades 3 and Up)

At the start of the school year, and again in January, or after the first, second, and third marking periods, pose this to your students:

Imagine that in June, there will be an assembly with all of the students in the school. The principal will call up every student and tell everyone what you will be remembered for doing over the course of this school year. That is called your legacy—your most important accomplishments by which you want to be remembered. I will give out index cards and I want you to write down what it is you would like the principal to say about you to the assembly of everyone in the school, at the end of the year.

Review the legacy statement at the end of December or at the end of the first (and second and third) marking period. Give the student another index card and ask, "What can you do to make it more likely that the principal will be able to read what you want?" This also is a chance for a student to amend/change what they said at the start of the school year.

Note: These "legacy cards" can also be useful in disciplinary situations. When students misbehave, they can be asked how they believe what they did will help them achieve their legacy at the end of the school year. Often, this cognitive dissonance helps students recognize their behavior is not in their longer-term interest.

Incorporate SECD Into Classroom Management

Even the best preventive efforts, of course, will not be 100 percent successful. Consequences for infractions should be clearly articulated, fairly applied, and, to the extent possible "logical." In phrasing a reprimand respectfully, you are not relinquishing authority or clarity. Rather, you are helping to de-escalate a problem, and modeling norms for dealing with conflict. When a student feels embarrassed by a teacher in front of peers, it is only natural for a "fight or flight" response to occur. There are no winners to any ensuing escalation or "fight", and while "flight" may appear on the surface to be acquiescence, it may be accompanied by lingering resentment and damage to relationships.

In SECD-building classrooms and schools, students learn and practice skills and techniques that can help them manage stressful situations and communicate effectively. Most SECD programs include ideas for building emotional regulation skills. The Social Decision Making/Social Problem Solving Program, for example, recommends helping students learn to "Keep Calm" through a process of (a) recognizing bodily reactions to impending stress; (b) identifying situations that put one at risk for poor self-control; and (c) establishing "Keep Calm" as a verbal prompt (with visual reinforcement around the classroom) to interrupt the fight or flight response with deep breathing and positive self-talk (see Chapter 6 for more details). With this approach, teachers would also help students learn and practice skills for "BEST" communication (as elaborated in Chapter 7). The acronym, which also serves as a behavioral prompt, stands for the four core components of assertive communication: Body posture, Eye contact, Saying appropriate things, and Tone of voice. Once conflicts have de-escalated, it is helpful to facilitate reflective discussion about the nature of the problem, the feelings and perspectives involved, and alternate, respectful and peaceful ways the problem could have been solved.

Skills such as Keep Calm and BEST redirect problem behaviors and help students develop their abilities to manage strong emotions and stress. Opportunities exist throughout the curriculum to learn and practice these skills. We have even found these and other SECD skills to be useful to educators in managing the everyday stresses of their work (see Chapter 6 for more on this topic). Because our approach to classroom management interconnects with the competencies addressed throughout this book, we will revisit the topic in more detail in Chapter 9.

Summary: Behavioral Expectations and Discipline Checklist

- ☐ Have students give input into a class "constitution," clearly post this, refer to it often, and use it as a springboard for reflection on communal behavior.
- ☐ Consistently enforce rules and reinforce positive behaviors.
- ☐ Use infractions or conflicts as opportunities to engage in problem solving and solution finding.
- ☐ When speaking with students about behavioral concerns, do this in a way that shows respect and does not embarrass them.
- ☐ Put into place a system to help students proactively prevent problem behaviors, such as a "cool down" zone for students to use when they experience strong emotions.
- ☐ Use the language of SECD when prompting positive behaviors.
- ☐ Establish a non-verbal sign for students to "get quiet," as opposed to shouting to be heard.
- ☐ Give students responsibility to make positive contributions to the class community, such as by playing roles as monitors, or helping to decorate.
- ☐ Introduce and practice self-control and communication skills.

Your Classroom's Climate

There are many inroads to promoting a positive class climate. Decisions educators make about everyday class transitions, pedagogy, and behavior management will have a meaningful impact on the learning that occurs in the class. You may already be doing things similar to those described above. Now would be a good time to review the checklists in the chapter. For each, consider: What ideas am I currently putting into place in my classroom? What are one or two ideas from each checklist that I want to try out over the course of the next month or two?

As you implement these ideas, what might you expect to see? To begin with, you will be creating a classroom that moves toward a vision of whole child education, in which all students are healthy, safe, engaged, supported, and challenged. Similarly, the New Jersey School Health and Climate Coalition (http://sel.cse.edu/new-jersey-culture-and-climate-coalition/) describes a learning organization imbued with positive climate, and these characteristics are easily applicable to classrooms as well.

A classroom with a positive climate is:

- Inspiring: The class community is guided by a shared set of values that serve as a constant reference point. Students and teachers take time to articulate a shared vision and core class values.
- Challenging: Classroom activities are differentiated to engage students at different levels and with a range of interests. Students have a voice in determining their own educational goals and shaping their learning experience.
- Supportive: Students know that they will get the academic, social, emotional, and behavioral support they need, and feel safe taking risks to overcome challenges. Students know that their opinions and perspectives are valued.
- Safe and Healthy: Promoting physical, social and emotional well-being is seen as everyone's responsibility. Students (along with teachers) are indeed their classmates' keepers, helping to problem solve and plan for prevention of problem behaviors.
- Engaged: Students have the ability to exercise choice and leadership in meaningful ways in the classroom. For example, students have the opportunity to lead traditional parent conferences.
- Respectful: Interactions among students and between students and teachers are marked by courtesy and civility. Students learn about one another's cultures (which can even be linked to the social studies curriculum!).
- Community of Learners: Students actively support one another as learners, and take responsibility for the growth of all class members. The class celebrates learning efforts and accomplishments, and students can nominate their peers and/or themselves for recognition of contributions to the class community.

The process of building a positive class climate is self-perpetuating; the creation of a caring community provides energy that propels progress in deepening relationships and learning. Small initial gains serve to sustain motivation for change. Students (and teachers!) come to take more pride in their work.

Reflections

This chapter contains ideas for structuring a classroom in a way that best promotes SECD growth and academic learning. A summary of major themes is included in Box 3.3. Before we begin exploring specific ways to infuse SECD into the curriculum, we suggest the following reflections:

- Which of your current classroom practices best support SECD growth and academic learning? What are the greatest strengths?
- What are the most notable shortcomings in supporting SECD growth and academic learning in your class? What has stood in your way of addressing these areas up to now? How might you overcome this?
- Which SECD elements do you yourself model most effectively in the classroom? What enables you to do so?
- What SECD elements are difficult for you yourself to enact as a model for your students? What derails your ability to model these? What are some steps you can take to build your own SECD skills in these areas?

Box 3.3. General Guidelines for a SECD-Enhancing Climate

1. **Be Aware of Your Own Feelings and Those of Your Students**
   - Share how you are feeling with students.
   - Ask them to label how they are feeling when positive and negative things occur.
   - Ask, "How else is anyone feeling?" or "How else might someone be feeling when something like this happens?"
2. **Show Empathy and Try to Help Students Understand Each Other's Points of View**
   - Empathy requires being aware of both one's own feelings and those of others.
   - Encourage students to reflect on how **others** feel at various times during SEL classes—when positive and negative things happen.
   - Ask, "Who else feels that Luis might be feeling that way? How else might he be feeling?"
   - Encourage empathy by asking students to help each other during and outside of SEL lessons.

3. **Keep Your Cool and Follow the 24-Karat Golden Rule of Education**
   - **Keeping cool**
     - Talk with students about:
     - Difficulties of keeping cool under stress.
     - How **you** try to keep your cool, and ask them to talk about how **they** try to keep their cool.
   - Shift discussion from people **losing** their cool to people **keeping** their cool.
   - **The 24-Karat Golden Rule of Education:** *"Do unto your students as you would have other people do unto your own children."*
     - Empathize with students' and staff members' perspectives.
     - Control your own impulses.
     - Know when you are overwhelmed and do not take this out on others.
     - Keep other people's strengths in mind.
4. **Be Positive and Help Everyone Keep the Big Picture in Mind**
   - **Be Positive**
     - Laughter is linked to our creativity and inventiveness.
   - **Big Picture**
     - We want students to think about how this will help them in life, school, or their future.
5. **Use Your BEST Social Skills in Handling Relationships**

   - Body posture
   - Eye contact
   - Saying the right words (Skipping the wrong words)
   - Tone of voice
   - BEST skills convey that we respect people and want to be with them.
   - Help students to develop BEST skills when they interact with each other.

Source: Adapted from Novick, Kress, & Elias 2002

Appendix: Classroom Constitutions

Sample 1

Bill of Rights and Responsibilities

Adapted from the work of Lorraine Glynn and her Sixth Grade Students at the Benjamin Franklin Middle School, Ridgewood, New Jersey, as published in Elias and Bruene Butler, 2005c.

STUDENTS

Article I

> Right: Students may use the classroom properly.
> Responsibility: Students must make sure whatever they use stays in good condition.

Article II

> Right: Students may place their belongings at a specific desk.
> Responsibility: Students must not touch another's belongings without asking.

Article III

> Right: Students have a right to express themselves without interruption or name calling.
> Responsibility: Students must listen and wait if they wish to share ideas.

Article IV

> Right: Students have a right to sit at their desks to do work.
> Responsibility: Students will not disturb others either physically (hitting, poking) or mentally (distracting by sounds or words).

Article VII

> Right: Students have a right to play computer games at designated times.
> Responsibility: Students must be finished with assignments and check with the teacher before playing. Students must share computer time with other students.

FACULTY

Article I

Right: Faculty have the right to expect students not to go into the faculty members' desks or other belongings.

Responsibility: Faculty must let students know what they can use and when they can use it.

Article II

Right: Faculty have the right to present the Topics they are required to teach.

Responsibility: Faculty must allow enough time for students to complete Topics and give whatever help is needed.

Article III

Right: Faculty have the right to be listened to during class without interruption and without insulting comments ("this is boring, stupid," etc.).

Responsibility: Faculty must allow students to express themselves equally, using appropriate behavior (speaking one at a time).

Sample 2

Norms adapted from the MOSAIC curriculum

- What is said in the MOSAIC Circle stays in the MOSAIC Circle.
- One person talks at a time.
- Right to pass—you do not need to answer the question if you do not want to.
- No dialogue—MOSAIC Circle is not a time for discussion; it is a time to share your own thoughts and feelings.
- Ask for help: You're not standing by and watching your school work get harder, you're taking action.
- Be a role model: Sometimes just doing the right thing goes a long way to set an example for other students.
- Help others: When someone needs help, go out of your way to help them out.
- Show respect for all people: Even when people are very different from you, you respect their rights and opinions.
- Take turns speaking.
- Participate actively in group tasks.
- Listen to each other.
- Respect each other.
- Encourage others to contribute and stay on task.

Chapter 4

Self- and Social Awareness

Background

In the CASEL 5 competency SEL framework, self-awareness and social awareness represent two different domains. While there are various statements of what comprises these domains, most accounts agree on the following:

Self-Awareness refers to:

- Feelings Vocabulary: Recognize one's feelings and thoughts and accurately label them.
- Feelings Awareness: Recognize the impact of one's feelings and thoughts on one's own behavior.
- Self-Appraisal: Recognize one's personal traits, strengths and areas of challenge.
- Self-Efficacy: Exhibit proactive self-confidence in handling daily tasks and challenges.
- Optimism: Look toward the future with positive expectations, including about the success of one's own actions.

Social Awareness refers to:

- Perspective Taking: Recognize and identify the thoughts and perspectives of others.
- Empathy: Recognize and identify the feelings of others.
- Understanding social/ethical norms: Demonstrate an awareness of the expectations for social interactions in a variety of settings.
- Respect for diversity: Demonstrate an awareness of the differences among individuals, groups and others' cultural backgrounds and demonstrate an understanding of the need for mutual respect when viewpoints differ.
- Social support: Recognize family, school, and community supports.

Of course, the first thing that might strike you is that self-awareness has a hyphen and social awareness does not. This is almost a literal reflection of how self-awareness is inward, all about us, and social awareness is about separateness, our relationship to others. We include them together within the same domain, for instructional purposes, because we see them as interrelated.

This is not a unique idea. About 2000 years ago, the ancient sage Hillel expressed this connection:

> If I am not for myself, who will be for me?
> And if I am only for myself, what am I?
> If not now, when?

What neuroscience has confirmed, Hillel already intuited: one cannot separate one's sense of one's self from one's connection to, and commitment to, others. Self-awareness without social awareness is, ultimately, selfishness. There is a pedagogical insight, as well. We learn self-awareness as a reflection from others. Individual neurobiological development is affected by a child's social and cultural contexts and networks of peer and adult relationships (Cantor, Osher, Berg, Steyer, & Rose, 2018). Understanding one's environment is inextricably connected to one's self-understanding. For children, it means that they first learn to recognize and name feelings in others before they are able to apply that process to themselves. Hence, the term "self-awareness." It's not that the child is not having feelings and reacting to them. It's that children first learn the labeling process in others. Of course, it's not accurate to describe these as sequential. Both processes are iterative. But from our perspective, the starting point is being able to accurately recognize what feelings look like in others, and then make connections to oneself.

So, Hillel had it right—being "for myself" means also being for others and having others be for you. To be only for yourself is not a normal, healthy, human condition. Hence, "What am I?" Clearly, not a person of character, not a "mensch."

As we look at how to build different skills, several other points are worth noting. First, we continue to appreciate the importance of emotion in everyday learning and behavior. The early SEL-related programs were largely cognitive and behavioral, and viewed emotion as a distraction of sorts from "rational" problem solving. Emotions were to be controlled, not understood as an essential source of information. With our new understanding of the role of emotion in all aspects of human functioning, it's clear that children need to understand how to accurately "read" emotions in themselves and others, as well as in different media, such as art, music, and literature. As children get older, we need to expand their emotional vocabularies as well as their ability to focus properly on emotions as situations get intense and emotional signals become more complicated.

Second, most consider *empathy* to be part of social awareness. However, we are making empathy the focus of the next chapter for pedagogical, not conceptual, reasons. In this chapter, we emphasize elements of empathy that are particularly closely connected to social awareness: *recognition of feelings in others* and the *effective listening skills* needed to communicate. In the next chapter, we focus on *gaining a deeper understanding of what might give rise to feelings* and perspective taking.

One's ability to detect how another person might actually be feeling (vs how you believe he or she might be feeling if you were that person) is basic to empathy. The use of the word "detect" is intentional because it requires some detective work to discern how others might be feeling. One must learn to look for cues, as well as decode them accurately based on culture, gender, and other contexts. It requires careful attention, knowing what to attend to, and persistence.

With regard to perspective taking, perhaps no one has done better work for longer than Robert Selman. He points out that perspective taking develops from egocentricity (my perspective is the only perspective, or at least the only one that matters) to being able to see another person's point of view, to being able to coordinate multiple different perspectives at once (as one must do in classrooms, families, and workplaces, for example). This is not a skill that children master, and indeed most adults are constantly working on it. Selman and Dray (2006) provide an interesting example regarding different pathways of perspective taking when a child is mistreated, harassed, or bullied by a peer (and it does depend on the peer context). Depending on a child's prior experience and his or her perception about the individual engaging in the behavior, he or she may be oriented to not put stock in the incident, or to respond directly about it. Even within those two broad choices, there are options; the ultimate choice is influenced by the ability of the child to accurately take the perpetrator's perspective (vs being primarily influenced by one's own feelings at the time). So, for example, a child who realizes the perpetrator is not out to get him in any way might just ignore the situation, or assertively stick up for himself; the situation might be the same, but another child who is feeling vulnerable and threatened for other reasons might not notice the context cues and might lash out angrily, or make threats to retaliate later.

Clearly, the ability to coordinate multiple perspectives—including one's own self-awareness—will influence the actions taken. Essential to this is accurately reading signs of different feelings in others, as well as having a sense of what someone else might be experiencing. Regardless, "knowing where others are coming from" is an essential component to effective social behavior in school, both with other students and with adults. And of course, the same applies to the adults, in interpreting students' behavior. Indeed, one of the greatest challenges to teachers is to be able to discern the perspectives of multiple students, every day for 180 school days each year. No wonder the profession is so taxing, even on an "easy" day!

Throughout this book, before we introduce specific activities related to the target skills—in this case self-awareness and social awareness—we'll discuss how everyday classroom routines can help set the stage for skill growth.

Setting the Stage for Self- and Social Awareness

A person is a person through other persons.

(Traditional quote associated with Ubuntu philosophy)

I see you, therefore you are.

(Based on a traditional Zulu greeting)

Norm Setting

One of the most basic applications of social awareness is the concept of norms. Norms are the answer to the question of how should we treat one another in our classroom and school, to preserve a sense of safety and respect and ensure that we can successfully go about the business of learning. The Northeast Foundation for Children's book "Rules for School" (Brady, Forton, Porter, & Wood, 2003)—part of the Responsive Classroom approach—clearly and thoroughly outlines a collaborative approach to establishing rules that include meaningful student input. By getting input from students, especially in middle elementary grades and upward, they are more likely to realize that rules are not meant to be punitive or restrictive, but rather, helpful. When students understand clearly what is expected and what is and is not acceptable, and the consequences they can expect when they violate the rules, they understand that discipline is not meant to be punitive. Still, to ensure that students do not feel punished when they suffer consequences, it's valuable to review the norms often and explain why they have been created. And the norms can be revisited when student behavior suggests that the norms are not effective. Finally, more and more schools are adopting restorative practices as part of their normative system. A number of resources exist to aid those interested in bringing in this deceptively simple process. We also introduced the idea of norms in Chapter 3 and provide more detail about behavior management and consequences in Chapter 9.

Both self-awareness and social awareness require students to have a feelings vocabulary that goes beyond the customary "mad," "happy," and "bored." Understanding the range of feelings in oneself and others is a building block of social-emotional competence/emotional intelligence. Below, we will describe activities for developing a feelings vocabulary. For now, let us consider how to make feelings part of the everyday routine. Teachers can decorate their classrooms with posters—possibly student-generated—about feelings. They can share their own feelings throughout the day. Students can be asked to do a feelings "check in." This can happen in many different ways. For example, in a Sharing Circle (as described in Chapter 3) students can be asked to share one word to describe how they are feeling. Or, students can use a magnet or popsicle stick with their name on it to indicate on a class feelings chart how they are feeling.

General Strategies for Self- and Social Awareness

We find it helpful to streamline the discussion into three categories of skills:

1. Having a robust feelings vocabulary and knowing how different feelings manifest non-verbally (and also how they feel in one's body; see Chapter 6).
2. Recognizing and respecting one's own beliefs and opinions and those of one's peers.
3. Understanding what situations and beliefs may lead to certain feelings; looking at the "causes" of feelings.

Expressing Feelings Verbally and Non-Verbally

We find that an effective strategy is to build up emotional vocabulary to describe situations involving others (whether actual or depicted) and then apply them to oneself. The following are suggestions that can be used, modified, or adapted to fit the specific developmental age and cultural context of your students. We have adapted these activities from examples across multiple curricula (Elias & Arnold, 2006; Elias & Bruene, 2005b, 2005a)

Feelings Memory Match Game (Primary Level)

1. Collect pairs of pictures of feelings based on faces of children, or drawn emoji-type figures. Feelings can include happy, sad, mad, angry, upset, surprised, excited, proud, unsure, worried, scared, nervous, silly, or jealous. For younger children, start out with four different, basic feelings and then add as they show mastery. Review the feelings with the students before playing and ask when someone might feel that way. For older students, consider allowing them to add one or two pair of feelings that they draw onto blank cards (or bring in pictures of those feelings).
2. Put out the cards feelings side down and mix them up. Have a student turn over a card and then try to turn over the matching card. If he or she gets a match, they take the cards out of the game and they get another turn. When they take off a match, ask the child to tell about a time they felt that feeling (to foster the other-self-awareness connection) and/or when they saw another person feel that way. This works with two to three students playing; if you are playing with a student, try to prolong

the game by "missing" matches. The student also can be the sole player and work with the goal of clearing the board successfully.

3. Continue several rounds. Don't emphasize who gets the most matches, rather focus on how quickly students (individually or multiple) can clear off all the cards.

Additional Activities (Younger Students)

- Read the Feelings First: Using storybooks, read aloud to students. Stop and ask students what feeling the character is feeling and how they know (what tells them the character is sad, mad, happy, excited, etc.)
- Feelings Guess Who: Help students learn to identify physical signs of feelings in others by showing pictures and asking them to guess what people are feeling. As a follow-up to this activity, ask students to pay attention and try to identify how people are feeling by their facial expressions *and* body language.

Feelings Jeopardy (Middle School)

1. Use a "Jeopardy" game format as a way to help students define emotion words.
2. The answers would be the definitions; the question would be, What is [a feeling]?
3. Examples:
    - Feelings for 100: Anxiety. Question: What is, when you are facing uncertainty or the unknown, or you are being confronted with something that you see as a threat to your happiness, comfort, social status, or physical well-being?
    - Feelings for 200: Hope. Question: What is, when I think about the future, you believe that good things will happen, even if you might be facing challenges right now?
    - Feelings for 300: Pride. Question: What is, when you feel happy, satisfied, and valued because of an achievement, quality, or skill—either yours or that of a person or group you care about?
    - Feelings for 400: Guilt. Question: What is, feeling that you broke an important rule or did not live up to an important value, especially a value held not just by you, but also by people you deeply care about or respect?
    - Feelings for 500: Betrayal. Question: What is, feeling foolish and hurt because someone you trusted told you a lie that you believed, or deceived you in some other way?

You can also create a Feelings Board Game (for example, similar to Monopoly, with properties consisting of feelings and the colors corresponding to groupings of feelings).

Additional Activities (Older Students)

- Feelings Charades: Divide the class into two teams. Give one student a flashcard with a feelings word on it. The student must act it out non-verbally while teammates try to guess what it is. Then the other team gets a turn. The goal is to see which team can recognize their actor's words most quickly.
- Mirroring: In this exercise, students demonstrate what feelings look like. Choose two students: one as the Communicator and the other as the Mirror. Explain that as you read the following scenarios, the Communicator will make a facial expression that reflects each feelings word. The Mirror's job is to copy exactly what the Communicator does.
  Sample scenarios:
  1. Jacquetta is excited about a gift she has just received and curious about what it could be. She becomes frustrated when she can't untie the ribbon, but finally opens it and is surprised to find it empty!
  2. Jose is worried about his dog, Spike, who has stayed out over-night. He hears a scratching sound at the door and is suspicious about what it could be. When he opens the door and sees Spike, he is joyful. But then he remembers how upset he was and becomes angry. But not for long!
  3. Angela is disappointed when a class trip is canceled but is happy when her dad suggests a movie that evening.
  4. A student is contentedly working on a math assignment when he encounters difficulty and becomes frustrated. After trying several solutions, he solves the problem and feels proud and satisfied.

Feelings Role Plays With Observations

There is great value to having students role play situations as a way of improving their awareness of their own feelings and those of others, and their ability to clearly verbalize both.

- Step 1: For each of the scenarios, select students to role play and prepare them to carry out the scene.
- Step 2: Designate some students to look for signs of feelings in the focal student in the scene and others to look for signs of feelings in the other student(s) involved. They should be prepared to write down what they see.
- Step 3: Act out a scenario, have the observers write their responses, compare them, and come up with a consensus.
- Step 4: After the scenario, while the observers are writing and discussing, have the actors in the role play write down their feelings and how they think they communicated them.

- Step 5: Have the actors share, have the observers share, ideally writing down the responses for all to see and reflect on. Discuss similarities and differences and why those might exist.

Sample Scenarios

1. You are the last one chosen for an activity.
2. You are part of a group and your peers ignore you.
3. You and friends are watching a school team play and they win.
4. An adult in the school yells at you in the hall, lunchroom, or on the bus.
5. Someone promised to bring something into school you need for an assignment and forgot for the third time.
6. Someone compliments you on something you did well.
7. You are walking down the hall in school and find a $20 bill.
8. You are asked to try out for a school team or performance group.
9. You are with some friends and you learn some bad news about a family member who is taken ill.
10. A friend says something that hurts your feelings.
11. A teacher comments on your work and says you probably can't improve it.
12. You study a lot for a test but get a disappointing grade.
13. You have an interview for a job in the school office/an after school program.
14. You arrive at school and you have not had breakfast. This is the third time this week this has happened.
15. Someone calls you an insulting name.

Feelings Freeze Frame

Overview: This tableau activity adds a new dimension to the role play activity and asks students to shift perspective. Students are asked to create a still life "snap shot" depicting a scene. The Feelings Freeze Frame focuses on the emotional dimensions of the scene. To develop further social awareness, the scene is recreated with students taking on different characters.

Step 1:   Choose your stimulus materials. These can be drawn from situations in stories, historical events, or hypotheticals based on the sort of situations that students encounter. The sample scenarios, above, can be useful (some will need to be adapted to include two or more characters).

For example, the following is an adaptation of scenario # 9:

Shondra is with two friends at recess. The Principal comes and shares some bad news about one of Shondra's family members who is taken ill.

In this activity, students work in groups. The number of students in each group should match the number of primary characters in the scenario to be depicted. In our example, we'll work with groups of four (for Shondra, two friends, and the principal).

Step 2: Assign or have students choose one of the characters in the scenario to represent in the Freeze Frame.

Step 3: Distribute or have students create a name card for their character.

Step 4: Explain the idea of a tableau to the students:

- In this activity, we'll be creating living freeze frame pictures of how the characters in [a story/historical event] may be feeling. I'll read you the scenario and then you'll have a few minutes with your group to plan out what your freeze frame will look like. Remember, you'll need to show how the characters are feeling without talking or moving.

- Review: Discuss with students how they can convey feelings without words or movement (e.g., through facial expression, posture).

Step 5: Read/tell the scenario to the students.

Step 6: Get students to work in their groups to plan their freeze frame.

- If there are many groups, you work with half the groups at once, with the others being spectators.

Step 7: Tell the students to create the tableau they planned. Make sure that each is holding their name cards.

Step 8: Discuss

- If you have designated some students as "observers," point to a tableau and ask volunteers to tell you how the characters are feeling, and how they know. Do this for several characters.

- If you are not working with observers, ask some of the groups to unfreeze and ask them to serve as observers.

Step 9: Mix it up!

- Ask the students to switch name cards with someone else in the group, so that everyone is now playing a different character.

- Repeat process of planning the freeze frames, showing them, and processing the portrayals of feelings.

- If there are multiple characters in the scene, you can repeat so that students can portray other characters.

Step 10: Connect to perspective taking

- Discuss how different characters feel differently in the same situation, and that their feelings are interconnected.

Learning About One's Self and Others

Self-awareness is about more than just feelings. It is also about recognizing one's tendencies, patterns, strengths, and preferences. In addition to being able to name feelings, it is important for students to become aware of their own opinions, values and beliefs, and those of their peers. Below are several activities designed to help do this. These activities provide opportunities for considering and expressing one's opinions and listening to those of others. Note that most activities involve many different SEL skills. The following are no different. They involve listening respectfully to peers' views. This requires strong social awareness skills, knowing one's own views, and being able to express them.

Identity and Purpose Interview

This interview procedure will allow students in Grade 5 and upwards to understand themselves and others. Adaptations can be made for lower grades, including having questions like #2, 4, and 5 in Table 4.1 answered using writing, interviews, or art modalities.

Step 1: Distribute the interview sheet in some format (we've provided a sample, below).

Step 2: Pair up students and have them interview each other and write down their responses.

Step 3: Have them write up their interviews and share with their partners for feedback.

Table 4.1 Identity and Purpose Interview Worksheet

1. What motivates you?	2. What are you good at? *Consider: Art, music, dance, cooking, science, reading, poetry, writing, athletics, building, fixing, talking to others, helping others, relaxing, singing, outdoors stuff, agriculture, etc.*
3. How do peers influence you?	4. When and with whom are you at your best?
5. Who do you turn to when you need help?	6. What is your strongest virtue and skill?

Source: Adapted from MOSAIC Curriculum, www.secdlab.org/MOSAIC

Step 4: Review student responses so you can prompt, encourage, provide relevant experiences, etc.

Step 5: Have students write in their journals what they have learned about themselves from this interview, including their strengths/preferences.

The Three Zones Activity (Younger Students)

Adapted from MOSAIC Curriculum, www.secdlab.org/MOSAIC

The Three Zones Activity is designed to help students become aware of their own beliefs as well as those of others.

Step 1: Explain to the class that the students will get a chance to reflect on important parts of their lives that most students feel strongly about and that often influence how we feel in many situations.

Step 2: Create three different areas of the room that will represent different responses. Make sure the three designated spots are nicely separated so students have to walk towards them. If there is spare paper and tape, you can attach the label of the designated spot to remind students what area they are in
- One area will be called "Mostly true for me"
- Another will be called "Partly true and not true for me"
- Last one will be called "Mostly *not* true for me"

Step 3: Read each sentence and ask students to answer by going to the designated response places and complete the steps below.
- I used to think school was pointless. But now I think school is important and I need to learn so I can succeed.
- I used to be violent in some situations. But now I am more peaceful and would only use violence where there is a real danger.
- I used to think that trying does not matter. But now I believe that the more I try, the more I can succeed.
- I used to do what would make me popular with others in school. But now I do what I want and what I think is the right thing to do.
- I used to be someone who just came to class to pass the time. But now I am someone who wants to be involved in the school and learn.

Step 4: After each question, ask students to explain why they are responding with their answer. At the very end have a discussion on what students think they need to work on and how they might be able to do it.

Note: Follow up can be part of improvement plans and/or written into students' notebooks or journals

Language Arts Extension

Ask students to complete the sentences below and write them. Connect any other instructions that would connect the activity to existing Language Arts curriculum priorities:

- I used to be...
- But now I am...
- I used to think...
- But now I think...
- I used to do...
- But now I do...

Allow students to share their own sentences with their classmates. Ask for volunteers to share some of their personal sentences about how they may have changes, using one of the "be," "think," or "do" stems, and explain them.

Three Zone "Yes-No-Maybe" Discussions (Older Students) (Adapted from the STAT Curriculum)

Yes-No-Maybe can be used often, as a "Do Now" activity to introduce a unit, start a Sharing Circle, morning meeting, or advisory, or respond to an assembly program or an incident in the school, community, or world. Note that all statements should be adapted to your own circumstances and curriculum units. Yes-No-Maybe is a good way to introduce "Big Questions" that are part of your units. We've provided some sample discussion questions below.

- Step 1: Introduce the activity: We are going to do something called "Yes-No-Maybe" that will involve moving around the room to consider our own and classmates' opinions on various topics.
- Step 2: Designate and label three separate spaces/areas in the room, one for "Yes", "No", and "Maybe."
- Step 3: Provide instruction: I am going to read a sentence and when I am done, you will move to the Yes, No, or Maybe spot of the room depending on whether you agree or not (Yes=agree, No=disagree, Maybe=not sure). If you agree and move to "Yes," you have to share one reason why you agree. If you move to "No," you have to share one reason why you disagree. If you pick "Maybe," you have to share both something you agree with and something you disagree with about the statement.
- Step 4: When students do move to the corners of the room, have them get into groups of three or four even within the same area. Have them

discuss why they said Yes, No, or Maybe. Even if all students have the same opinion, there will still be various reasons for those opinions and those will broaden students' perspective taking and overall social awareness.

- Step 5: After students have shared opinions in subgroups, have a spokesperson for each subgroup share the consensus of their ideas. There is no comment or feedback on what students share, only clarification questions as needed.
- Step 6: Repeat as you wish to include other Yes-No-Maybe questions.
- Step 7: If you have time, have students take their seat and ask, "Was there anything that surprised you during the activity?" Again, the point is to have sharing and listening, not to reach any conclusion. An effective closing statement is to point out, "You had many different thoughts and there was not a single right answer."

Sample Statements About School Issues

- All schools should have metal detectors so all students and staff can feel safe.
- Cheating does not affect anyone unless they get caught.
- It's okay to criticize someone on social media if you don't say their full name.
- When a new student comes into the school, they should be taught to go over to other students and introduce themselves.
- It is not the responsibility of students to clean up the cafeteria at lunchtime.
- Whether someone smokes or uses drugs is up to them and no one should force them not to.

For a Unit on Manifest Destiny

- There was no other way for the United States to grow, but to expand west.
- Native Americans were right to fight against colonization of their lands.
- Manifest Destiny was necessary to the success of the United States as a nation-state.

For a Unit on the Civil War

- Many other countries had slaves; what the United States did was no different.
- It's not right to take down statues and change streets named after generals and others who fought for the South in the Civil War.
- President Lincoln freed the slaves so that they could fight in the Northern army.

For Language Arts, Science, the Arts

- The author of the book we just read should have written a different ending.
- There is no good reason to send astronauts to the moon or to Mars.
- I think a symphony should have all fast movements.

Understanding My Character Strengths

A key part of self-awareness is identifying areas of strength, as well as areas to improve. This feedback can be used to make improvement plans, but also just has value in building students' self-understanding. It is helpful to have a set of virtues on which to build. In Chapter 2, we highlighted three such approaches. As students share their strengths, they are also building social awareness by learning about those of their peers.

In general, it is useful to ask students in groups to discuss virtues, individually select one or two that they feel are their strengths, as well as one or two areas they would most want to improve (they can ask for feedback from classmates), and then have someone be in charge of summarizing the totals for each group. These should be recorded on a white board or large post-it so all students can see the results, and kept visible as a reminder of strengths and areas of potential improvement. Teachers should note that some students' strengths are others' areas need improvement and teachers can formally or informally encourage those with strengths to help those seeking to improve in those same areas.

The activities below build on the character virtues used by the MOSAIC program (www.secdlab.org/MOSAIC).

Define the Virtues (Developed for Middle School)

a. Provide students with a list of virtues and potential definitions (Box 4.1).
b. Have them work in groups—from one list—to match the virtues to the definitions; the virtues will have at least one definition.
c. Once groups arrive at a consensus, ask them to share results and justify their choices. You will find that while it may seem obvious to you, there might be differences of opinion and the importance is in having students explain their reasoning and listen respectfully to their classmates' opinions.
d. Follow up by asking students for times they have observed others showing any of the virtues in school or outside of school; ask them to share situations where they exhibited one or more of these virtues, or could have, but didn't.

e. Assign students to use one, two, or more of these virtues in upcoming writing assignments

f. Have them write essays about what one or more of these feelings means to the student, using whatever essay writing format your language arts curriculum is teaching now.

Box 4.1. Define the Virtues

Directions: Match 2–3 definitions (bottom) to the Virtues (top).

Helpful Generosity
Optimistic Future-mindedness
Responsible Diligence
Compassionate Gratitude
Forgiveness
Constructive Creativity

A. Thinking "outside the box"
B. Giving things (like money/games/fun) to others without expecting anything in return
C. Finding new solutions to problems
D. Being dependable (people can count on you)
E. Moving on after something bad happens
F. Giving love, kindness, time, appreciation, or help to others
G. Working hard and getting your work done
H. Thinking about how your actions affect other people
I. Setting goals for your future
J. Sticking with it and not giving up, even if times are hard
K. Having a hopeful outlook or being optimistic
L. Looking at something in a different way from most others
M. Not holding a grudge against others

Opinion: What Is the Most Important Virtue?

Introduce this activity by connecting it to optimism. Talk to students about how you believe that everyone has a positive purpose in life, by which you mean something they have a talent for and are meant to do. A big part of going to school is finding out what your strengths are and what your positive purpose might be. Consider self-disclosing that your positive purpose is being a teacher, being there for this class and helping your students learn what they need to grow up well, be good people, and make valuable, positive contributions to the world.

Step 1: Ask, "Which of these virtues is most important to finding your Positive Purpose?" There is no right or wrong answer!
   a.   Optimistic Future-Mindedness (growth mindset, hopeful aspiration)
   b.   Responsible Diligence (resilience, perseverance)
   c.   Helpful Generosity (service, civic/school engagement and contribution)
   d.   Compassionate Gratitude and Forgiveness (get past negative circumstances, see the positive side)
   e.   Constructive Creativity (seeing many paths, being innovative)

Step 2: Place Students in Groups
Place students in groups based on the most important virtue they identified.
   a.   Groups should be 3–4 students.
   b.   If a student is the only one to select a virtue, have them make a
   c.   second choice.
   d.   It's okay if some virtues are not represented.
   e.   It's okay if some virtues are represented twice, i.e., in two groups.

Step 3: Provide Instructions for Groups to Defend Their Chosen Virtue
Instructions for Groups: Students will work together to write down why their virtue is the most important.
   a.   Ask students to identify a note-taker for the group. Have students brainstorm reasons their virtue is more important than the other virtues.
   b.   Example: Optimistic Future-Mindedness is the most important because without it, you could not use the other virtues to plan for the future.

Step 4: Have students present their opinions and have other groups listen respectfully.

Note: In coordination with Art and Music classes, students can create and/ or identify artwork or songs that are examples of their preferred virtue. Displays or presentations can be made of these, including to parent or community groups. This all helps to elevate these virtues in students' thinking and as guides to their behavior every day.

Effective Listening

Part of being aware of others is to be attentive to them. In our increasingly distracted digital age, when many believe the myth of multi-tasking, many of us try to do something else while purporting to listen to someone else at the same time. Our students are increasingly likely to fall into this habit. This activity, a variation of which can be found in many SEL curricula (e.g., Second Step, www.secondstep.org), is best used with grades 3 and higher.

- Step 1: Ask students if they have ever felt that someone was not listening to them when they were saying something important. Then, make a list of all the things they noticed as examples of not-good listening skills (e.g., someone not facing you when speaking to you, doing something else at the same time, like texting, speaking at the same time as you are, someone not responding when you have finished saying something). You may want to model, in an exaggerated and humorous way, the suggestions students make.
- Call the list something like, "Poor Listening Skills" or "How to *Not* Listen Well" and refer to it when you see examples of it in the classroom.
- Step 2: Now create a parallel list of good listening skills, focused on the question, "How can you tell when someone is really listening to you and cares about what you are saying?" The list should include such things as looking at the speaker, facing the speaker, non-verbally reacting to what is being said, and asking a question about what was said. Obviously, this will be adjusted to the age of the student.
- Step 3: Pair students and have one talk about something he or she enjoys or did recently that was fun, for 30 seconds. Set a visible timer if possible. While the student is talking, ask the partner to model good listening skills. Then have them switch. Ask students to give each other feedback on how they felt they were listened to.
- Step 4: Repeat (either with same or different partners) but this time, ask students to model poor listening. After each student has a turn, have a class discussion about the differences in the two examples, highlighting how they felt when they were not listened to.

    Note: Consider pairings that reflect diversity, such as boys with girls and students from different nationalities/backgrounds. Repeating this activity periodically, whether the positive or negative modeling, will in the course of time help students continue the ongoing process of developing better listening skills.

Self- and Social Awareness in Language Arts

Language arts is particularly fertile ground for developing self- and social awareness. On a most basic level, feelings words can be included in vocabulary lists. Further, there are now many lists of books that introduce students to a range of feelings at an appropriate age. Two such familiar stories are "The Cat in the Hat" and "The Lorax," both by Dr. Seuss. Keep these stories in mind as you review the lesson planning sequence below. One of our favorite books for use with children in grades K-1 is "The Way I Feel," by J. Cain, also published in Spanish as "Así me siento yo." This story introduces young children to numerous feelings they may experience, using wonderful rhyming text and colorful illustrations. The board book covers silly, scared, happy, sad, thankful, jealous, disappointed, frustrated, angry, shy, bored, excited, and proud and the situations that can lead to these emotions.

The Reading Feelings Activity (Adapted from Bruene Butler, Romasz-McDonald, & Elias, 2011)

Step 1: Tell the group that today you are going to read them a story about many, many feelings. But before you read, you want to show them the pictures. For each of the pictures, ask what feelings the students see. Ask them how they can tell. Note: This will be a diagnostic activity for you, to see how well your students are attending to signs of different feelings and how this improves over time (and where it might not, for the group or for individual students).

Step 2: Tell students that when you read the story, you would like them to make an appropriate feelings face when a feelings word is encountered in the story (e.g., when the work, "happy," is read, the students should all show a big smile). Note where students might miss a particular feeling and help them look at classmates so they can get it right.

Step 3: Review. Ask students what feelings they remember from the story. Make a list. If possible, ask students to volunteer to try to draw a face next to each feeling on the list.

Step 4: Ask students to tell about a time when they have felt each of the feelings.

Step 5: As a supplement or alternative to drawing feelings, bring in magazines and have students cut out pictures that show different feelings. You may want to make arrangements with local medical professionals or hair or nail care professionals or others in office situations where there are magazines, so that you can get a supply before they recycle them. Make the point to your students that feelings are all around us, in movies and TV shows, posters and billboards, literally everywhere. Their job is to notice. Another option is to create worksheets with lists of feelings and spaces for students to paste or tape pictures they have cut out that correspond to those feelings. We've included an example (Table 4.2). This might be an excellent activity to coordinate with an Art teacher, for integration into the Art curriculum.

Step 6: Give your students periodic opportunities to share feelings they have noticed, both what and when/where.

Table 4.2 Feelings All Around Us Worksheet

HAPPY	**SAD**
PROUD	**ANGRY**
SILLY	**NERVOUS**

Related Activities for Grades 3–4

Tell the class that you are going to read them a situation and their job is to pick a "Feelings Square" that shows how they would feel if that situation happened to them. You can use situations that are happening in the classroom, school, or community as well as those listed below.

Prepare feelings squares (or have students do so) with these feelings at least:

Lonely, Happy, Sad, Puzzled, Jealous, Excited, Nervous, Angry, Proud

Read the situation and ask students to volunteer (or select them) to pick a Feelings Square that they think corresponds to the situation. Ask them to show what the feeling looks like and then explain why they chose it. Afterward, ask if anyone else would have chosen that, and why. Then, make the point that not everyone will feel the same way about situations, and ask if anyone would pick a different square. Follow up as before.

Situations:

- You get a good grade on your homework (proud, excited)
- You want to play with someone but all of your friends are doing their homework (lonely, sad)
- Your friend, sister or brother broke your favorite toy (angry, sad)
- Your pet is sick (sad)
- You really want a game that your friend has (jealous, angry)
- You are going to a birthday party (excited)
- You are invited to join a club at school (proud, excited, nervous)

Self- and Social Awareness for Educators

Everyone working in a school brings their experiences with them every day. Some of these are emotion-laden, and these are likely to affect us in ways we can't always anticipate. However, by exploring our own emotional reactions and being aware of them, the strong feelings that different situations might evoke will be less likely to surprise and/or derail or overwhelm us. Stern, Hyman, and Martin's (2006) work provides excellent guidance in this area, some of which is summarized below:

1. Listen to your own internal dialogue. Be aware of your trigger situations, when you are at your best/worst, biases, and stereotypes. Notice how you feel after different situations, especially when you feel you handled something particularly well or poorly, regardless of what the specific resolution was. Sometimes, doing the right thing does not yield success, and we can solve a problem but not feel good about how we did

it. Use these feelings as a sign to review what happened and what else can be done differently.

2. How effective am I at identifying a range of different feelings I experience as events are taking place? Retrospectively? What strategy can I use to stay calmer and be more aware in my feelings in the moment?

3. Use a version of the Trigger Situation Monitor, used with students, to help monitor both positive and negative responses and learn from both kinds of situations.

4. Keep a journal to regularly reflect on, and record, responses to important emotional awareness questions, such as these:

    a. Why am I reacting to particular students in particularly emotional ways? What from my own life and past is being activated?

    b. Do I favor some students over others? Do I find myself avoiding some students? Do I avoid certain kinds of professional situations? What patterns do I notice in this? What is my plan for corrective improvement?

    c. What kinds of stories and situations do I react to most emotionally? Why? Does this bring me helpful insight or hinder me?

    d. What strong emotions did I experience today? What was the situation and who else was involved? How did I manage my emotions? What strategies can I use to better manage my strong feelings in the moment?

Self-Reflection: Self-Knowledge Guide to Personal Action Planning

- Reflect on how you learn best. For example, you might learn best by teaching; if so, seek out opportunities to present to others. You might learn best through quiet reflection; if so, find this quiet time.

- Reflect on how you best let your caring show. For example, find people in your school to mentor, help your colleagues get to know each other better, or extend your relationships beyond the school. What are appropriate ways to let your students know you care about them?

- Reflect on how you stay grounded despite stress. For most, it helps to make it a priority, no matter how busy you are, to stay in contact with your friends. They are your fuel.

- Reflect on how you know when enough is enough. There is always more that can be done, for a project, for a colleague and of course, for our students. Set guidelines to help you move on when appropriate/ necessary.

- Reflect on how much you build celebration and recognition into your work at school. How do you help others feel accomplishment even when they may not have been successful? Reflect on how much you appreciate recognition of effort and consider how to help colleagues and students also feel that appreciation.

- Reflect on your own strengths and work preferences. What is the best praise you ever received? How often do you like to check in with your colleagues, supervisors, administrators? What is your best method for building relationships? How do you learn best? Consider asking your colleagues these same questions to promote their own reflection.

Chapter 5

Empathy and Perspective Taking

Background

In the previous chapter, we focused on elements of social awareness—recognizing feelings in others and effective listening—that are closely linked with empathy. In this chapter, we'll deepen our exploration of empathy, and discuss perspective taking—*understanding why someone might be feeling how they do* and *trying to see situations from the other's point of view.*

Despite how often empathy comes up in our conversations with educators, researchers and theorists seem to spend a surprisingly large amount of effort trying to figure out what the term even means! Most begin by pointing out the Greek roots of the word: *em + pathy = feeling + in* (or into), meaning that empathy has to do with one's emotional experience being in tune, or in sync, with another person's. The term "emotional empathy" is often used to describe this aspect—feeling sad when another is sad, frightened when another is frightened. Empathy, in this sense, is a sort of small-scale emotional contagion.

Neuroscientists have entered the discussion by positing a role for *mirror neurons* in creating a basis for what seems like an automatic, second-hand emotional response. When one observes the activity of another person, the observer has a neuronal response not only in the sensory areas involved in perceiving the activity, but also in the neuronal system that parallels that being used by the person conducting the activity. I see you kick a football, *my* neurons related to football kicking light up. Some researchers have pointed to the presence of mirror neurons in the areas of the brain responsible for emotional reactions. If these neurons respond to the emotions of others by creating parallel neuronal activity, then one would, arguably, "feel" what the other is feeling.

When educators say they'd like students to show more empathy, though, they are talking about much more than emotional mimicry or contagion. *Ethan cries. Missy cries. Janet cries. Everybody cries.* We don't imagine the teacher is delighted at this mass exhibition of empathy; in fact, he may be ready to cry himself!

What's Missing?

Missy and Janet have become fully immersed in Ethan's experience; they've lost themselves in the emotions of the other. Martin Buber (1878–1965) was a philosopher who considered this problem. Living in Germany during the rise of Nazism, and, as a Jew, facing increased discrimination, he witnessed what happens when we come to see others as objects, there to be used and controlled. Buber referred to such relationships as "I-It." I'm a person; you're an object. In "I-Thou" relationships (to Buber, it was *ich-du;* today we might say "I-You"), in contrast, individuals meet as equal partners. Real dialogue and understanding become possible. Buber emphasizes the importance of the *I* along with the *Thou.* "So, while it is crucial to learn and see and feel from another's perspective, it is equally important to approach difference in a way that does not result in dissolving difference by losing one's own voice in the dialogue" (Shady & Larson, 2010, p. 87). Buber emphasizes "the capability to experience the other, to 'swing into' (*'einschwingen'*) his or her reality, and, at the same time, experience one's own reality" (Schmid, 2001, p. 57).

When talking about emotional mirroring, it is easy to move from talking about "feeling with" someone else to assuming that we "feel the same way" as that person. Take Dr. V. S. Ramachandran's (Marsh, 2012) claim about the potential connection of mirror neurons and empathy. Dr. Ramachandran helped to discover mirror neurons and is, not surprisingly, a major proponent of their potential.

> If I really and truly empathize with your pain, I need to experience it myself. That's what the mirror neurons are doing, allowing me to empathize with your pain—saying, in effect, that person is experiencing the same agony and excruciating pain as you would if somebody were to poke you with a needle directly. That's the basis of all empathy.

But can we *really* experience the "same agony?" Would this be adaptive, in an evolutionary sense? Is this why lunchtime and recess in many schools are out of control? Even on a neuronal level, the strength of the mirrored response is only a small proportion of that of the original. Moving away from neurons, things get even more complex. Our emotional reactions are determined by the contours of the situation and by the personal and cultural identities we bring with us. A child of recent refugees may be frightened upon entering a new classroom. His peers' mirror neurons may be signaling this emotion. But, as Buber suggests, there needs to be acknowledgement of both a commonality of experience and a uniqueness. I might feel (a scaled-down version of) the student's fright, but there is much more to that student's experience than "feeling with" can tell me. Everyone brings unique context into their interactions. To assume that one knows anyone else's feelings and perceptions in minute detail actually has a name: egocentrism. It's not a desirable attribute.

In promoting empathy, we often prompt students to think about times that they have been in parallel situations or experienced similar emotions. This seemingly basic technique raises important caveats about identity and interpersonal (mis)understandings. Mattie is sad and scared because her mother's military unit is being sent to a combat zone. Leo's parents are not in the military, but he has felt sad when his mom goes away on business trips, and was even frightened once when she came home late from the mall. Does Leo's experience provide him with an in-depth understanding of what Mattie is really going through? Most unlikely. In fact, even if Leo's mom *was* in the military and had been deployed, could it really be assumed that he is feeling *the same* as Maddie? Would their gender matter? Their relationship with their parents? The presence of others in the home? Their prior experiences with deployment? The experience of their friends and relatives around deployment? There is also a risk of assuming that Mattie "must" feel that way because "all kids of deployed parents" feel that way. Though perhaps done with the best intentions, this inches toward stereotyping: All [members of group X] feel [emotion Y] when they are faced with [situation Z]. Yes, Mattie is a member of group X. And, she also is Mattie.

These caveats shouldn't deter us from pursuing the empathy equation. Psychologist Irving Sigel, whom we discussed in Chapter 2, spoke of development as an ongoing process of fine-tuning mental representations (e.g., Sigel, 1993). The way we construct our world is necessarily incomplete—there is always more to learn that will help shape what we know, how we feel, and what we do. Our learning about the experience of the other can be seen as helping us shape a more nuanced understanding of the experience that person is going though. Cognitive empathy—what we might call perspective taking, or understanding another person's point of view—complements emotional empathy and brings us closer to experiencing the situation of the other. Closer to, yet necessarily still not fully. But closer is important.

Empathy involves emotional awareness and cognitive perspective taking, and goes beyond these. *"Jamie is sad. So what?"* or *"Jamie is sad and it's bumming me out, I'm outa here"* isn't what we're aiming for. Educators' interest in empathy includes a behavioral element in addition to the affective and cognitive. That is, we want the emotional reaction and our cognitive assessment of its causes and context to shape our behavior. Of course, action without emotional and cognitive perspective taking doesn't meet our needs either: "I want to make Jamie feel better so I will make funny faces" [though Jamie is sad because of a recent death in the family, and funny faces would not be appropriate].

Empathy = Shared feeling + Understanding perspective + Motivation to act + Appropriate Action

As with all SECD competencies, empathy does not stand alone; it relates to other skill areas. Empathy hinges on the ability to read the emotions of another person, as discussed in the previous chapter. Responding out of empathy calls on problem solving and decision-making skills (Chapter 8). Importantly, our empathy equation is related to emotional self-regulation. An empathic feeling of distress may result in a full-fledged distress reaction, as in our earlier case of our crying contagion. One's patterns of handling emotionality play a role (Eisenberg, 2000).

Setting the Stage for Empathy

It should be clear by now that getting to know "the other" is perhaps the most important element of empathy. Building community in a classroom, as discussed in Chapter 3, is a necessary step.

Getting to Know One Another

Taking the perspective of "the other" involves *knowing about* that person's experience. To Hoerr (2018, p. 86), "Empathy comes from listening and learning about others' situations and feelings in order to understand their perspectives. It's seeking to understand values and rationales, going beyond 'What do they think?' to '*Why* do they think that?'" We'd add: Going beyond "What do they think *and feel*" to "Why do they think *and feel* that." We can't know that Maddie is sad because her mom's military unit is being deployed without knowing that she has a mother in the military and that her mom's military unit is being deployed and, ideally, something about Mattie's past experiences with deployment. Knowing about Maddie as an individual is crucial. We know what we know about others by honing our ability to understand and infer their perspectives and emotions. We will build on activities in the previous chapter to show you how to help students develop this ability.

Scaffold Naturally Occurring Empathy Opportunities

How we respond to our students' emotions can model—or fail to model—empathy. Think about the following scene.

> Ariel looks upset. Her body language is droopy, her eyes are red. This is unusual for her.

As an educator, you...

a. Do nothing. Kids are moody she'll get over it.
b. Tell her, "Smile Ariel, it can't be that bad."
c. In front of the whole class, say "Ariel, what's up today? You look miserable."
d. Privately, ask her how she is feeling and what's on her mind.

Picking (d) is a great start. Let's continue with the scenario.

> TEACHER: Ariel, the look on your face and your body posture make me wonder if something is bothering you. What's on your mind?
> ARIEL: Nothing…it's stupid. My dog is really sick and may be dying.

OK, your turn again. Do you respond:

a. You're right. That is stupid. It's only a dog.
b. Do you think your mom will let you get another?
c. Would it cheer you up to be the board monitor today?
d. I'm so sorry to hear that. How are you feeling?

Again, we'd recommend (d) as an example of focusing on the feeling.

The other choices can be considered restrictive teacher language, which is "direct, controlling, impersonal, and indifferent" (Mugno & Rosenblitt, 2001, p. 69). The truth is, time and pressure will lead even the best of us to sometimes not choose (d). Responses (b) and (c) are attempts to make things better fast, which often make sense in our moments of hecticness with multiple demands on our time from multiple students, etc. But these other responses won't work because they don't address the feeling involved. They are responsive to the situation, but not the emotions at play. Emotionally responsive teacher language, in contrast, "conveys respect for and acceptance of an individual's feelings and ideas, encourages give and take, implies choices, and provides elaboration" (Mugno & Rosenblitt, 2001, p. 69).

Emotionally responsive teacher language recognizes the need to go beyond what I think a child may be feeling, or "should" be feeling, to actually understand more about what that child actually is feeling in this particular situation. And we do this by asking a little bit more and reflecting on what we are seeing and hearing as the child responds. All this, of course, within our time constraints. This is empathy, not therapy. However, our slightly deeper inquiries often can tell us whether bringing in a school support staff member might be a good idea.

Empathy Awareness Breaks

Further, everyday classroom activity provides opportunities for educators to take an empathy awareness break, to stop action and bring to the surface emotions that are frequently experienced in a situation. Jacobson (2017) provides an example from the work of Facing History and Ourselves, a SECD initiative that uses historical examples of genocide as a jumping-off point to fostering intergroup acceptance, as implemented in the John Adams Middle School in Santa Monica:

> On the day after Halloween, eighth graders stand in a large circle, preparing to read a line or two from the scary stories they have been writing.

But before they start, Beeman-Solano [the language arts teacher] asks them to consider why some students groan when asked to read their own work before the class. "It's embarrassing," one student says. "Fear of judgment," another says. A third responds, "Some people could feel anxiety or stress in public speaking."

According to Mary Hendra, a staff member at the Facing History program, "Pausing for such a discussion helps the students remember how to be respectful audience members and reinforces a central Facing History principle of 'putting yourself in somebody else's shoes'" (Jacobson, 2017).

General Strategies for Developing Empathy

In this chapter, we build upon the work of social awareness introduced previously and focus on *understanding why someone might be feeling how they do* and *trying to see situations from the other's point of view.*

Feelings Detective

Social awareness includes not only correctly labeling feelings in others but also understanding why they might be feeling that way. We'll dive deeper into this in the next chapter. To know someone is sad is important, yet interacting with them in a proper way typically is aided by knowing something about what might have led to the feelings observed. This is especially true in culturally diverse contexts.

Here is an activity that is aided by pictorial props appropriate to the age, gender, and ethnicity you might like to highlight for your students.

Step 1: Prepare pictures (from the Internet, magazines or other sources) depicting common situations. For example, a student sitting alone in the lunchroom; a student waiting in line; a group of students dejected after an event; students high-fiving.

Step 2: Questions for each picture:
- What feeling or feelings do you think the student might have?
- Why might the student be feeling that way?
- What might have happened before, leading up to this picture?

Note: This is an activity best done first with the whole class and a very simple emotion, so they can understand the task and create varied stories that might apply. Clearly, as students get older, the emotions depicted can get more sophisticated. Many SEL programs have guidelines regarding developmental displays of emotion; general guidelines are available from the work of Carolyn Saarni (2007). (Adapted from SDM/SPS materials Bruene Butler, Romasz-McDonald, & Elias, 2011; Elias & Bruene Butler, 2005c, 2005b, 2005a.)

While you can continue to do this with the whole class, it is also helpful to have students do the task individually when they can write it, and then share in groups so they can understand how different classmates might react differently to both the feelings displayed and the stories created. When you find students "miss" some obvious cultural/economic contexts (such as a student looking sad because he or she might be hungry or homeless or might have a relative who is in danger), you can interject these possibilities along with explanation, and consider adding relevant literature to your curriculum. Similarly, if you do cover some ethnic or cultural or even historic content, you can use a variation of this activity to check to see your students' understanding of possible feelings.

When processing the group sharing, remember that there is not always a single correct answer for the feeling or for the explanation; in fact, almost *never* for the latter. Unless there is an egregious mis-attribution of feelings (e.g., happy for enraged), it's best to acknowledge possibilities. Social awareness in an increasingly globalized world is aided by being able to consider a range of reasons for people's feelings (creating the need for more and more accurate communication, a skill we focus on later), as well as appreciating that not all people express the same feelings in exactly the same way. Hence, the need to attend to BEST attributes (see Chapter 7).

Understanding Other Points of View

The following activity takes the idea of standing in another's shoes to a literal level!

FIG Footsteps (Adapted from Elias & Bruene Butler 2005b)

Overview: This activity provides students with an opportunity to switch perspectives physically while they do so in their thinking. It is a concrete way to work with empathy and perspective taking. The activity can be adapted to multiple age groups and content areas.

To get started, you'll need:

- Unlined paper, 2 sheets per person.
- Scissors (optional).
- Markers/crayons/other art supplied (optional).
- A scenario in which two individuals see things from different points of view.

The basic idea is for students to create footprints in which to stand when they are in their roles. When it comes time to switch perspectives, the students literally go to stand in the shoes (okay, shoe prints, but close enough) of their peer to reflect back what they heard and to check for understanding.

Step 1: Choose your stimulus materials. These can be based from situations in stories, historical events, or hypotheticals based on the sort of situations that students encounter.

Step 2: Introduce the idea that everyone has a different *point of view.*
- Use a very concrete example. Point out that when you look at the class you see faces, they see backs of heads. Hold up objects and tell how what you are seeing differs from what they are seeing.
- Point out that people also have different points of view about things they like, or things they want. Ask about, for example, students' favorite ice-cream flavors to demonstrate that what some people like, others don't like.
- Explain that sometimes when people have different points of view they may get into an argument about their disagreement and they need to solve their problem.

Step 3: Introduce FIG (or review it):
- For this activity we're going to focus on taking someone's perspective while working through the first three steps of decision making and problem solving. These are:
  F-Find the feelings
  I-Identify the problem
  G-Guide yourself with a goal

Step 4: In this example, we're going to apply FIG to a hypothetical problem. We've included a scenario here; feel free to create your own or use something from the curriculum!
- Hypothetical scenario: *Hannah and Kyle are put in charge of planning an activity for the class to do together as their part of the annual holiday festival assembly. Each class gets 5 minutes to do something of their own planning to be performed or presented to the entire school, and every class wants their plan to be awesome! Hannah wants the class to present a song about celebrating together with family and friends—some kids would work on the words (which will be sung to a popular tune), some would work on dance moves. Everyone in the class would sing and dance together at the assembly. Kyle wants to present a mural dedicated to people in the military who will be overseas during the holiday. Each student will work on a part of the mural on a very large sheet of paper. At the assembly, the class would show the mural, and some of the students would explain what it is about. After the assembly, the mural would hang in the classroom.*

Step 5: Process the scenario
- Ask students to think about Hannah's FIG:
  - What might Hannah be Feeling?
  - What is the problem you've Identified for Hannah?
  - What does Hannah want to have happen; what is her Goal?

- Repeat for Kyle's FIG
- Repeat from other examples that the students generate based on different points of view in class, or from the curricular content.

Step 6: FIG Footsteps Role Play

- Ask students to trace their feet on pieces of paper, making "footprints" for themselves and, if you'd like, have students cut these out. If you want, give students an opportunity to decorate their footprints.
- Use the handout in Box 5.1, or write the steps on the board.
- Explain to the students that in this activity they will actually be standing in the other person's footprints in order to practice seeing things from another point of view.
- The students will work in pairs. Assign one student in each pair to play the role of Hannah and the other Kyle. Explain that they will tell their partner how their character is feeling, and listen when their partner explains how their character is feeling.
- To get ready, ask students to stand in their footprints facing one another. Prompt students to take a deep breath and think about the activity, then review these instructions.

Box 5.1. FIG Footsteps

Everyone has a point of view. The way we see things can make a difference when we're trying to work out a problem. This activity will help us look at issues from different points of view.

Directions: Trace shoes and cut out pairs of shoe prints using the pattern. In pairs, students stand on their footsteps. One student presents their side of the problem using the language below (Step 1). The other student listens, and then "steps into" the speaker's footsteps and paraphrases back what they heard (Step 2) using the language below. The original speaker clarifies as needed. Each student returns to their footsteps. Repeat Steps 1 and 2 for the other student. When this is done, students make suggestions for compromise until a solution is reached.

Get ready!	Take a deep breath and focus.
Step 1	I feel... I think... I want...
Step 2 (repeated with return to Step 1 as needed)	You feel...Is that right? You think...Is that right? You want...Is that right?
Step 3	How about if...

FIG Footsteps Role Play Instructions

ROLE PLAY PART 1

- Using the prompts, each character takes a turn explaining their feelings, identifying the problem, and describing what they want to have happen.
- When they are done, the students should wait for your signal.

ROLE PLAY PART 2

- *On your signal*, the students should switch positions so that they are now standing in their partner's footprints.
- Using the prompts, the characters take turns explaining what they heard from their partner, and asking if they understood correctly.
- If there is a misunderstanding, the students should make appropriate clarifications.
- When they are done, the students should wait for your signal.

ROLE PLAY PART 3

- *On your signal*, the students should go back to their original footprints.
- Using the prompt, they should brainstorm for ways to resolve the problem that best achieve their goals.

Provide other opportunities to practice.

- This can also be done in a large group, with two volunteers asking their FIG, and the entire group helping to generate possible solutions.
- When two students are having a conflict in the classroom, you can "drop the feet" and put out two sets of footprints for each student to stand upon, as a prompt and cue to use FIG to constructively and non-violently solve the problem. You can distribute footprints to other staff members to use with your students as well, and explain their use. This can be invaluable at lunch, recess, and during PE.

Building Empathy Through Literature

The plot of most, if not all, of the literature students read—at any grade level—involves personal decision making and interpersonal conflict. Characters—from the Berenstain Bear family to the animals on George Orwell's farm—experience anger, joy, fear, and jealousy. They are faced with decisions both small and large. How do Pa Berenstain and his kids deal with Ma's observation that everyone is watching too much television? How will the animals react when Napoleon the pig descends into despotism? When we teach these books, we might focus on the narrative arc, how the characters develop emotionally and how their understanding of others, for better or worse, ends up influencing how they resolve problems.

We recommend strategic use of the proverbial "pause" button in order to dwell in and learn from those experiences of conflict. Help the students understand the characters' perspectives, feelings, motivations, and desires. Let them think about the options available to the character at various moments during the unfolding action, given what is known about the characters, plot, and setting up to this point in the book. While enriching students' appreciation for the decisions the characters eventually make, these pauses provide opportunities to enhance empathy.

Once you've hit the pause button and an emotional plot element is left dangling, one possibility is to lead a discussion about the characters' feelings and their point of view. For example, Naftel and Elias (1995) recommend the following questions:

- If you were [character] how would you feel?
- Are there any more feeling words to describe what [character] is feeling?
- Has anyone ever felt this way?
- What do you think [character] might be thinking right now?

If more than one character is involved, the discussion can be repeated from each character's point of view. After the discussion, the class can move ahead with their reading.

Literature, Empathy, and Social Studies

Monobe and Son (2014) recommend using global literature to deepen understanding of other cultures by seeking out authors "that authentically reflected individuals and communities without stereotyping or romanticizing the experiences of minorities" and "that represented voices and perspectives of children, who are immersed in political conflicts and/or war" (Monobe & Son, 2014, p. 70). They also sought out authors who are "(1) committed to writing about children or people who are underrepresented in the United States or globally, (2) were originally from the country, or (3) were inhabitants of the country for a significant length of time" (Monobe & Son, 2014, pp. 69–70). They provide examples such as *Brothers in Hope* (about refugees in Sudan) and *My Name Is Sangoel* (about a Sudanese family relocating to the United States).

Once a book is selected, these authors recommend that teachers:

1. Explore universal themes with students (often best in small groups, which can then compare perspectives) in order to help students "find a common ground" (p. 72).
2. Describe their own experiences (teachers' own, students' own, or both) with those themes, and compare and contrast their experiences with those described in the book.

Literature can be a particularly useful entry point to an understanding of the experience of immigrants (Mabry & Bhavnagri, 2012). Based on their research, they make recommendations that can enhance our general discussion of using literature to help promote empathy. They point out that participatory activities are important complements to discussion-based analysis of literature. For example, in studying a book (*A Piece of Home*) in which the protagonist must choose what to pack for a journey, the teacher asked students to symbolically pack a box with what they would take if they were placed in this situation. In other examples, teachers asked students to keep reflective journals from the point of view of the protagonist of the story.

They recommend that "teachers ask students to (1) write in the first person as though they are the protagonist, (2) to make personal connections between their life experiences and that of the protagonists, and (3) respond to specific questions from prompts related to protagonists' thoughts, feelings, and situations resulting in empathy and taking their perspective" (Mabry & Bhavnagri, 2012, p. 52).

Empathy and History

The FIG Footsteps activity, described above, can also serve to scaffold dialogue between historic personages. As in literature, our study of history is often a matter of understanding the challenges that individual face and the way they solve them given their historical context.

Historical empathy is a concept defined in multiple ways. It can describe considering how historical events affected those living at the time. In this way, it can serve to deepen understandings about the causes and contexts of decisions made by people at different historical periods. It can also indicate emotional engagement with both the past and the present—caring about the situation of people in the past and being able to apply lessons from history to contemporary life (Barton & Levstik, 2004; Endacott & Brooks, 2013).

An interesting example can be found in the Place Out of Time (POOT) project, and its off-shoot being run in Jewish religious schools (JCAT-The Jewish Court of All Time, Katz & Kress, 2018). In this on-line history simulation, students adopt the persona of historical figures in order to debate a "case" that is based on actual historical or current events. To navigate the simulation, students need to understand *their own* opinions and to think about how their characters might have reacted.

In a recent iteration of this program, students were asked to consider this scenario in which two French teenagers—one Jewish and one Muslim—sued the French government over its ban on head coverings. In November of that school year, while the simulation was running, a series of terror attacks took place in Paris. This provided an (unfortunate) opportunity for the intersection of feelings of self and others. A student playing Coco Chanel, the fashion designer who was also a French patriot with the resistance to the Nazis, comments that these attacks have hit me hard, when I heard about the news I started crying. I have spent almost my whole life living in France but the fact that the whole world is lighting up and showing their support for France. It is nice to know that people care.

Students picked up on the simulation's promotion of empathic perspective taking. When interviewed (out of character) by researchers, students made comments alluding to "feeling in somebody else's shoes and to be able to talk to them." Another student provided a particularly well-stated synopsis of perspective taking, stating that participation in the game provided "the knowledge of what people that think differently than me think about" and "the ability to see a problem from more than one perspective."

Empathy and Educators

As with other SECD competencies, educators who practice empathy themselves are better situated to develop this in their students. Given the nature of discourse—online, on news broadcasts —that denigrates other points of view and belittles those that hold them, the adults in the room are themselves at risk of empathic slippage. Even those who loudly espouse empathy and mutual understanding—and even regularly practice these—can be drawn into wondering how in the world "those people" could support a particular politician or policy. An empathic response requires a reframing of the question as one of inquiry and not bewilderment. *Why do some people support a particular cause or position?* is not in and of itself an unreasonable question—as long as it is seen as an opening to learning about others.

It is important for educators to be aware of the assumptions they make about why students (and peers, parents, etc.) do what they do, particularly when they are not doing what we want them to do. Fahy, Kupperman, and Stanzler (n.d.), studying the POOT program described above, share an anecdote about a graduate student mentor in a simulation in which students take on the roles of historical figures and engage in online discussion in character. One student's postings consistently contained spelling and grammatical errors. The graduate student's reaction was to wonder whether the student, known only as "Napoleon," actually cared about the assignment. After all, he/she didn't take the time to run a spell check! Eventually, Napoleon's teacher wrote to the team to inform them that the student had a severe learning disability and that the postings were actually the result of laborious, caring work (even with their mis-spellings) on the part of this motivated student. The graduate student reports learning to "not pass judgment on someone or a situation until you know the whole story." Once the full story was known, this student reports that "my thoughts went from telling him to use spell check to 'wow, that is amazing that he is participating in POOT and we should commend him on his work.'"

There are also activities for educators to do—during faculty meetings or elsewhere—to understand one another's point of view. For example, writing in Educational Leadership, Hoerr (2018) suggests that faculty be presented with controversial topics (Hoerr suggests Common Core Standards or Homework on Weekends) and asked to think of three reasons why someone might support each side of the controversy. Then, in small groups, teachers share their opinions and the reasoning behind them, and compare and contrast the actual reasons with those speculated. "The goal (which you'll need to state and, likely, restate) isn't to change minds, but to offer a forum for folks to explain why they hold their beliefs—and for others to listen and learn" (Hoerr, 2018, p. 87). This activity can also be done as a version of the Footsteps or Three Zone activities discussed in this and previous chapters.

Finally, an activity such as the Feeling Walking Tour (Box 5.2) can provide insight into how different members of your educational community feel throughout their day.

Box 5.2. Visualization Exercise: A Feelings Walking Tour

Imagine yourself taking a walk through your school building. Look in on classes, lunch and recess times, meetings, extracurricular activities, after-school and evening events—the entire gamut of what occurs on regular school days.

- Be aware of your feelings at different destinations on your tour.
- Where do you experience positive emotions, such as pride, joy, and excitement?
- Where do you experience negative emotions, such as anxiety, frustration, and anger?
- Where do you experience both types of emotions?
- What might be happening at these times and places to cause these emotions?
- Think about the experience of students and/or other teachers in these destinations. It is quite possible that they may be experiencing some of those same emotions. How might this help you better understand their decisions and actions?

Source: Adapted from Novick, Kress, & Elias 2002

Chapter 6

Self-Regulation

In the previous chapters, we focused on self- and social awareness and empathy, the ability to recognize and understand the emotions, beliefs, opinions, and values of one's self and one's peers. But knowing how one feels is only one element in the complex dynamic of social interactions.

I am feeling [fill in the blank…jealous, fearful, elated, etc.]. Now what!?

Students bring their emotions with them into the classroom. They may be distracted by events at home, or something that happened on their way to school. They may be on edge from not having had enough sleep or food. They may be lovestruck because the object of their affection waved to them in the hall (or deflated because they didn't wave).

The school day itself presents constant emotional ups and downs—conflict with a peer, elation at hearing about a class trip. Some assignments may seem rote and boring, others challenging and frustrating. And the school schedule doesn't help. School starts early. Lunch is scheduled when it is scheduled, whether or not anyone is hungry. The bell rings whether you are done with your work or not. Transitions may not make sense, leaving one taking an hour break for intense exercise in PE at 10am, sandwiched between quiet reading at 9am and a big math test at 11am.

Somehow, in the midst of all of this, students (and teachers!) need to maintain momentum even in the face of strong emotions that may seem distracting. The term self-regulation captures the ability to handle these emotions and to stay oriented toward one's goal. The use of the term has evolved over the course of our work. Early on, we often talked about *self-control*, and this is still a resonant element of the conversation. Daniel Goleman's book *Emotional Intelligence* (1995) popularized the idea of "emotional hijacking," that when we encounter strong emotions—the sort that call for a fight or flight response—we tend to go into a sort of emotional and behavioral auto-pilot. We react first and think later, if at all. The notion of self-control speaks to the need to manage these situations because our reactions—kicking a peer out of anger, running out of a classroom due to test anxiety—may actually be harmful to ourselves and others and not exemplify the virtues that we want to guide our lives and the lives of our students.

Self-control has come to be seen within a larger notion of self-regulation, a term used to describe "the ongoing, dynamic, and adaptive modulation of internal state (emotion, cognition) or behavior" (Nigg, 2017, p. 361) that one applies to one's self. More commonly, we use the term to describe the ability to focus despite distractions, either external (e.g., excessive noise) or internal (e.g., a strong emotion).

Sometimes, self-regulation is criticized as being about emotional suppression, negating feelings to always stay on an even keel. This is far from the truth. Our goal is not to create emotionless automatons. Rather, we want to help students understand their own emotional experience and the emotional demands of particular situations and to develop strategies to achieve congruence between the two. In a slogan fit for a motivational poster (and, in fact, this is where we encountered it!) —we want to have our emotions, we don't want our emotions to have us!

Fear, for example, can be instructive in highlighting danger; it is not a "bad thing," per se. Sometimes we even seek out fear (seen any scary movies lately?). But fear that inhibits performance during a test or a class presentation is an example of the mismatch between an emotional reaction and what is called for in order to handle a situation in a way that is most beneficial to ourselves and others. This involves a shift in mindset away from blaming a student for problem behaviors emerging from strong emotions. Fleeing the class as a result of intense anxiety may not be what we'd like to see, but it is understandable as a reaction to an intense emotion for which one has no other coping strategy. We want to provide coping strategies that are more productive! We also point out that the emotion-situation mismatch can work in the other direction; we might want a risk-taking adolescent to at least be more aware of the dangers (if not "fear" them) of their behaviors.

Self-regulation is not limited to those emotions commonly considered "negative," though we realize that the behaviors associated with these emotions, like the squeaky wheel, get the most attention. An emotion-situation mismatch can also occur with excitement, joy, or similar "positive" emotions. Many teachers notice challenges with self-regulation setting in as excitement builds prior to a school vacation, for example. In this case, too, the emotion is not "problematic"; the subsequent inability to focus is. We also take a broad approach to what is being regulated. So, while it is possible to think about cognitive, emotional, and behavioral regulation independently, we embrace the interdependence of these elements.

There are important steps that a teacher can take to set the stage for successful self-regulation.

Setting the Stage for Self-Regulation

A positive, warm student-teacher relationship, particularly during the younger grades, helps promote student self-regulation. "[A] teacher who is sensitive and responsive to her students may teach behavioral self-control implicitly through her interactions with her students" (Merritt, Wanless, Rimm-Kaufman, Cameron, & Peugh, 2012, p. 154).

We recommend that this implicit instruction be complemented by more explicit efforts to scaffold self-regulation. Self-regulation strategies should become part of everyday classroom language. Reminders will help students implement strategies; repetition and reflection will help them internalize these strategies.

Make More of Modeling

The school day presents teachers with nearly constant self-regulation challenges. Later in this chapter we discuss some self-regulation strategies for teachers to use for themselves. Those instances in which teachers put these strategies into action to regulate their own emotions can become teachable moments for students. Feeling stressed and rushed because an unexpected assembly left you with only a quarter of your instructional time? Go ahead, take that deep breath to refocus—and let the students see that you are taking that breath. Explain what you are doing and why you are doing it.

An Ounce of Self-Regulatory Prevention

Take a proactive approach to what Stanford researcher James Gross refers to as "the most forward looking" (Gross, 2015, p. 7) category of self-regulation strategies, *situation selection* and, relatedly, *situational modification*. Such strategies involve arranging the environment to be less likely to provoke self-regulation problems. While there are distractions that are beyond a teacher's control, there are many steps that can be taken to create a less distracting environment.

- Get to know your students' triggers. What are those sometimes idiosyncratic events that set them off? Often, a teacher can see these coming and take action to intervene. Below, we'll discuss how to help students understand *their own* triggers.
- Attend to transitions, as these can present self-regulatory challenges. Together with the class, take a few deep breaths before shifting from one activity to the next. Start the day with a check-in or Sharing Circle (Chapter 3) as a transition into learning.
- Post the day's schedule (if you work with young children and others with limited reading skills, you can use pictures). Review it with the students both at the beginning of the day, and as you move through what

is planned ("We're up to recess. After recess we'll be having Math"). Make sure that students are aware of changes to the routine and mark these prominently on the schedule.

- Schedule challenging activities (such as exams) when students are more physiologically "awake" and not immediately after lunch.
- Think about classroom layout that, when possible, provides space for focused, "quiet" work removed from "noisy" group work.
- Take "Brain Breaks" as described in Box 6.1.

Box 6.1. Brain Breaks Activity

Step 1. Introduce Brain Break Activity
- *"Today, we are going to take a Brain Break. We are going to do an **activity that will help your brain work a little better**. It's something you can try before a test or any situation where you want to be as alert and thoughtful as possible."*
- *"Scientists around the world have come to understand that our brains are affected by what goes on outside them."*

Step 2. Lead Brain Break 1
- *"I will call out the instructions for you and keep a count for you."*
  1. Gently tap the top of your head with your fingertips 12 times.
  2. Gently tap the sides of your head with your fingertips 12 times.
  3. Gently tap the back of your head with your fingertips 12 times.
  4. Tap the tops of your shoulders with your fingertips 8 times.
  5. Grab your right shoulder with your right hand and rotate your arm backwards 4 times. Then, rotate forwards 4 times.
  6. Grab your left shoulder with your left hand and rotate your arm backwards 4 times. Then, rotate forwards 4 times.

Step 3. Lead Brain Break 2
- Repeat the same "Brain Break" process.

"This time, as you are doing the Brain Break, be sure you are inhaling through your nose, breathing out through your mouth, and smiling while you are touching your head, shoulders, etc. Smiling is very important because it increases the flow of oxygen to our brains, which helps us be more creative and optimistic.

Step 4. Brain Break Debrief
- *Did you feel any different between the first time and the second time you had a Brain Break? How did you feel different?*
- *Tell students to ask for a chance to do Brain Breaks before tests or any situation where they want to be at your most alert.*

Follow up
- Arrange for Brain Breaks to be given before standardized and other testing.
- Be sure other staff members know about Brain Breaks; perhaps they'd like to try them as well.
- Consider using Brain Breaks to begin faculty meetings or staff committee meetings or professional development sessions.

Source: Adapted from the MOSAIC Curriculum

A General Approach to Promoting Self-Regulation

Self-regulation is most effective when it is preventive and not reactive. Calming one's self down from a very strong emotional reaction is so difficult that it might even be perceived as impossible.

CHILD: [crying and screaming].
TEACHER: OK, Jamie, just calm down.
CHILD: I CAN'T CALM DOWN!! [continues crying and screaming].

We all recognize the futility of this teacher's intervention (though we've all fallen into that trap!). We take Jamie at her word. Her emotional hijacking is so all-encompassing that it shuts down any rational thought that might guide her attempts to self-regulate. When there is a complete "meltdown," we are left trying to minimize its impact.

The best way to deal with an emotional hijacking is to avoid one to begin with. But how do we help students recognize that a meltdown is around the corner? Our strategy, adapted from materials from the Social Problem Solving/Social Decision Making approach (Bruene Butler et al., 2011; Elias & Bruene, 2005b), involves helping students (a) recognize the physical "early warning signs" that their body uses when reacting to stress and (b) anticipate situations in which they are more likely to face challenges to self-regulation.

Feelings Fingerprints

Feelings have physiological manifestations. We're all familiar with smiles and tears. There is a physical dimension to the intense emotional experiences that accompany an emotional hijacking in which our fight or flight responses are engaged. The term "autonomic response" —referring to the autonomic nervous system—is commonly used to describe what happens (though, technically, the culprit is the sympathetic nervous system, one component of the autonomic nervous system). When this system is engaged by threat, it prepares the body to react by moving blood around to where it is most needed, and away from where it is not. This is a "whole body" response; multiple organs and systems are mobilized. And, as blood moves around and systems come online or go offline, as it were, we experience these changes in our body in response to threat. Feeling warm? No surprise, given the blood rushing to your extremities to provide the oxygen needed to fight or flee. Tensing up, balling your fist, grinding your teeth? Your muscles are preparing for action. A bit nauseous? Perhaps it is due to digestion—not immediately needed to counter short-term stress—taking a break. Breathing fast or hyperventilating? Your blood is stocking up on oxygen to use as energy. (A note to biology and health teachers: the biological basis for autonomic over-arousal can be connected to numerous points in the curriculum.)

Although we all share commonalities in the functioning of our autonomic nervous system, we've found that people are particularly attuned to noticing at least one of its manifestations. We use the term "Feelings Fingerprints" to indicate that the experience of the onset of autonomic hijacking will differ person by person, but we all have these experiences. Feelings Fingerprints becomes the language for understanding the signs that one is "at risk" of autonomic over-arousal.

To introduce the idea that our bodies give us clues to when we are experiencing strong emotions, and that different people experience these differently, the Feelings Fingerprints Activity can be helpful.

Feelings Fingerprints Activity

Step 1: Ask students if they've ever heard of the term "butterflies in my stomach," and if so, what it means. Use this to introduce the idea that there are ways that our bodies feel when we experience emotions. We call these Feelings Fingerprints.

Step 2: Share your own Feelings Fingerprints: Use imagery to drive home the body sensations. For example, "a group of tap dancers in my forehead" or "my face gets as hot as the sun."

Step 3: Ask a few students to share their Feelings Fingerprints.

Step 4: Distribute a blank outline of a human body, as in the sample in Figure 6.1. Ask students to indicate using drawings how they experience their Feelings Fingerprints. Ask students to share their drawings.

For Older Students: Feelings Fingerprints can connect with material from Biological Science classes. Art classes can also focus on drawing one's feelings in a more complex way.

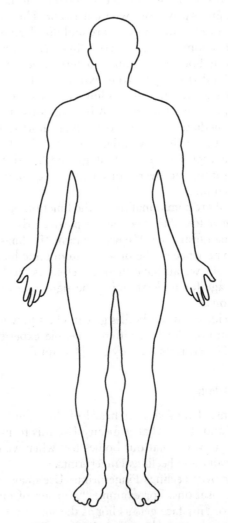

Figure 6.1 Feelings Fingerprints: How does my body tell me when I have a strong emotion?

Button Pushers

There is often some predictability as to what might set our students—and ourselves—off, what might push our buttons. While we acknowledge that there are some universal button pushers (persistent poking in the ribs comes to mind), there are also, as with Feelings Fingerprints, a lot of individual differences. What might seem innocuous or mildly annoying to one student may be a button pusher for another. Jordana starts sweating when she is rushed, while time pressure brings out the best in Elise. Elise feels sick to her stomach when she needs to give a presentation, while Jordana thrives in the spotlight (as long as she is not rushed).

Knowing about upcoming button pushers allows for preparation. Rather than helplessly watching the minutes tick down, feeling a growing knot in her stomach before her turn to present to the class, Elise can recognize the Feelings Fingerprints, associate it with the upcoming stress and take the actions needed to regulate her emotions. Perhaps she can distract herself by listening to music when she first starts feeling anxious. Or, perhaps she will find it useful to rehearse her speech one more time. The most important thing is for the student to have a proactive strategy that derails the train that would otherwise be barreling into the emotional hijacking zone.

The activity below, and the accompanying worksheet, can help scaffold a conversation about situations in which one is at-risk for emotional hijacking. As an example:

Introducing "Button Pushers"

Step 1: Review and connect to Feelings Fingerprints:
- "Who can remind our class about what we mean when we say Feelings Fingerprints?"
- Give examples of situations that make it likely for you to experience Feelings Fingerprints in the classroom. Ask students to share their situations.

Step 2: Describe the idea of Button Pushers
- "Just like we each have different ways for our bodies to tell us that we are losing our cool, we also have different things that push our buttons. Does anyone know what we mean by that term, pushing our buttons? [wait for student response and continue as needed]. Things that push our buttons are things that really bother us. Not just make us a little annoyed but make us start having those Feelings Fingerprints that let us know we are losing out cool. For me, for example, [insert example from your own experience]."
- Make it clear that everyone has situations that are more likely to lead to distracting emotions, even the teacher!

Step 3: Develop rationale for importance of identifying Button Pushers, draw from student experiences.

- "Can someone share a time they felt that their buttons were pushed and that they started to lose control. What did you do? What happened as a result? If you knew ahead of time that you were getting into a Button Pusher, what might you have done differently?"

Step 4: Introduce the Button Pusher Worksheet (Figure 6.2)

- "Before we start our work today, we're going to spend a few minutes thinking about some of the things that might push our buttons when they happen in this class. Please think about the question on the worksheet, and then write or draw an answer. You won't need to share your answer with the whole class if you don't want to."
- Once students have had time to write, ask for a few volunteers to share.

Step 5: Wrap up and planning

- "We're going to learn some strategies to help us keep our cool when we get our buttons pushed. For now, can I hear some ideas for what you might do when you get into a situation that you know might push your buttons?"
- Reflect and Review in future Sharing Circles
  - "Who can remind us of what a Button Pusher is? Has anyone found themselves in a button-pushing situation in the past week? What did you do, or what could you have done, in that situation?"

When do I find it hard to stay calm?

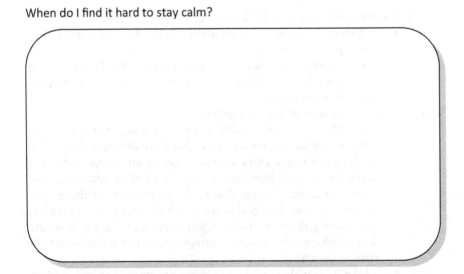

Figure 6.2 Button Pushers Worksheet

Keep Calm

Feelings Fingerprints and Button Pushers help us recognize that we are at risk for losing our cool. Now we need a strategy to avoid doing so! There is very little direct intervention that we can take to reverse the effects of the autonomic nervous system (as its name says, it is an autonomous system!). As much as one might like to get their blood flowing back to their stomach so they can finish digesting their lunch, they'd be hard pressed to actually accomplish this. Our breathing is a notable exception; we are able to speed up or slow down our breathing as we please. Of course, the more "hijacked" we are, the harder it will be to do so. Again, proactive steps are needed. Feelings Fingerprints and Button Pushers provide the early warning signals to provide intentional override to our mounting autonomic arousal.

Because our breathing is an autonomic function that we can, with relative ease, learn to intentionally control, it provides an opening for intervention. As noted above, breathing exercises are often part of mindfulness or contemplative approaches. Breathing is used as a focal point, to draw attention to one's current state of arousal. As crisis looms, breathing can also serve as a distraction to the avalanche of negative thoughts that feed, and are fed by, autonomic arousal.

Keep Calm was developed with this in mind and can be used as a prompt for taking alternative action to avoid emotional hijacking.

The four steps of Keep Calm are:

1. Tell yourself to STOP.
2. Tell yourself to KEEP CALM.
3. Breathe slowly while you inhale through your nose to the count of 5 and exhale slowly to the count of 5. Then, do it again.
4. Praise yourself for a job well done.

Each of these steps has a specific rationale:

Tell yourself to STOP.	Along with interrupting the physiological elements of autonomic over-arousal, we want to derail the cycle of negative self-talk that often accompanies such situations. We do this by substituting alternative talk: aloud for younger students and/or when starting out with the skill, eventually to be internalized.
Tell yourself to KEEP CALM.	As with all skills, we aim to develop a name and prompt that can enter everyday classroom talk. Keeping in mind that when Keep Calm is successfully implemented, the outcome could be "invisible." What we'd observe is a student *not* getting upset under conditions that would otherwise have set them off. So, creating a prompt that can be internalized as part of the skill itself is particularly important.

Breathe slowly while you inhale through your nose to the count of 5 and exhale slowly to the count of 5. Then, do it again.	As noted, deep breathing is a commonly used self-calming strategy.
Praise yourself for a job well done.	While we always seek to reinforce students' use of SEL skills, we also want to internalize that feedback. Again, this is particularly salient for self-regulation, where use of the skill may not be apparent to an observer.

What follows are the basic guidelines for a lesson around Keep Calm that can be used in the context of multiple content areas.

Keep Calm Lesson Outline (4th Grade), Adapted from Elias & Bruene 2005c

Step 1: Develop rationale
   a. Review prior lessons.
   b. Discuss with class: It is easier to handle challenges when you are calm. Illustrate with situations—in students' lives, in your own experience, and/or using examples from literature or history from recent class work—in which problems were exacerbated by lack of a calm problem-solving approach.
Step 2: Introduce the Keep Calm skill
   a. Discuss that athletes and performers use deep breathing as a way to calm themselves before and during events.
   b. Ask if students have come across this idea before or have noticed what players and performers do before they start.
   c. Tell the class that you are going to share with them a way to calm themselves down, and it's called "Keep Calm."
   d. Introduce the four steps of Keep Calm
      i.   Tell yourself to STOP.
      ii. Tell yourself to KEEP CALM.
      iii. Breathe slowly while you inhale through your nose to the count of 5 and exhale slowly to the count of 5. Then, do it again.
      iv. Praise yourself for a job well done.
   e. Demonstrate to the class, describing each step as you go. Explain that talking and counting to oneself is part of the slow breathing process that makes Keep Calm work.
   f. Have students practice, while you provide feedback. For example, you can ask them to run or jump in place for 10 seconds. Then say, "Use Keep Calm," as a prompt for them to practice. Repeat once or twice.

Step 3: Plan, Prompt, and Practice

    a. Re-establish content area connections by asking students which of the literary characters and/or historical figures previously discussed in class could have benefitted from using Keep Calm.

    b. Connect to students' experiences by asking them to anticipate when they might find it helpful to have used Keep Calm. Emphasize the usefulness of Keep Calm as it connects to success in the classroom; e.g., helping to stay focused when distracted; calming nervous feelings before tests.

    c. Use the term "Keep Calm" as a prompt throughout the day, as situations within content areas and within the classroom present themselves (e.g., walk the class through Keep Calm before an exam; role play Keep Calm using two fictional literary characters who are having a conflict).

    d. Post the Keep Calm prompt, and the four steps of the skill, in the classroom.

    e. Use Keep Calm within bullying prevention and other such initiatives.

Step 4: Follow Up

    a. To help Keep Calm take root, check in with students as a group and/or individually about their use of Keep Calm. When did they use it? When might they have used it but didn't?

Some suggestions for younger students

- To illustrate the idea of breathing deeply and calmly, ask students to demonstrate how they would smell a pizza. Use "smell the pizza" as a reminder to breathe deeply and calmly.
- Have students help decorate posters with Keep Calm prompts.
- Introduce Keep Calm in conjunction with spelling or vocabulary words such as feel, calm, and anger.

Some suggestions for older students

- Weave the use of Keep Calm into peer mediation and conflict resolution programs.
- During science class, discuss the biological basis of the "fight or flight" response.
- In science or math class, practice graphing measures of pulse (taken at the wrist) when students are stressed and when they are calm.
- Have students introduce Keep Calm to "buddies" in younger grades.
- Connect deep breathing with yoga and meditation, which may be familiar to some students.

Practice Keep Calm in situations in which stress is predictable; for example, before exams or when a student needs to present in front of their peers.

Look for opportunities in literature to discuss the Feelings Fingerprints and Button Pushers of characters in stories or personages in history and current events. In creative writing, ask students to describe their own Feelings Fingerprints, or those of a character they create for a story.

Addressing Dysregulators

> Doors slam shut. Voices and footsteps echo in the halls. Announcements come over the PA system. The room is too hot. The room is too cold. The space is crowded so people are getting in each other's way. The garbage gets picked up, the lawn gets mowed, the street gets repaved... all right outside your classroom window.

So far, this we've focused on elements of self-regulation that have to do with preventing unwanted behaviors that might result from overwhelming emotions. A student may, for example, use Keep Calm before replying to a barbed comment during an argument with a peer, rather than responding in kind. Self-regulation also encompasses the more workaday challenges of maintaining motivation under trying circumstances. These elements of self-regulation relate to the concept of grit, which, thanks to the exciting work of Angela Duckworth (2016), has become a common term to describe perseverance in the face of obstacles. Consistent with our overall strategy, we see grit as resulting from the successful application of social and emotional skills, and the creation of conditions favorable to the implementation of these. The discussion of motivation is related to that of self-calming. A request (demand?) to persist in tasks that one finds unmotivating can itself be a button pusher. Without skills for coping, pushing a student to "just plow through" an intensely boring or frustrating task can lead to a fight or flight response.

Being able to self-calm has multiple advantages. It prevents problems from escalating. It can also lead to a change in self-perception; it may help one "alter how one thinks about one's capacity to manage situational demands (e.g., 'Although making [a presentation] feels overwhelming, I know I can handle it using the techniques I've learned'") (Gross 2015, p9). Also, self-regulation can allow someone to enter, or remain in, a problem-solving mindset, focused on a goal related to what caused the self-regulatory challenge to begin with ("Now that I am not panicking about tomorrow's big game, I can get back to practicing my free throws").

While occasionally using Keep Calm will itself be sufficient to handle the situation, in most cases Keep Calm will not directly address the problem that challenged one's self-regulation to begin with. We find it helpful to break our approach down into two components:

1. Take immediate action to counteract the emotional hijacking that sets off unwanted responses.
2. Plan a strategy to handle the presenting situation.

These components support one another. If I begin to lose my temper because my classmate is tapping incessantly on his desk, to handle the situation I'll need to avoid losing my temper and starting a fight. I may avoid losing my cool, but my problem persists. The tapping is still getting on my nerves. However, I can now deal with it more effectively; my emotions are a signal of my need to find solutions to a problem.

No matter how well-designed the learning environment may be, and how well we are able to self-regulate, distractions are inevitable. We recommend being proactive in working with students to anticipate and handle such situations. Doing so may require problem-solving skills, as described in Chapter 8. For now, the Dealing With Distractions Activity below (adapted from the MOSAIC curriculum) provides a framework thinking about dysregulators.

Dealing With Distractions Activity

Step 1. Introduce the concept of self-management.
- Have a conversation based on these questions:
  - "How often do you feel distracted?"
  - "What are some reasons you lose focus?"
  - "Is it hard to complete tasks such as homework because of distractions?"
- Summarize by saying that self-management skills can help reduce distractions and keep you focused!

Step 2. Facilitate a discussion about distractions. Have a discussion about when it can be dangerous to lose focus and be distracted (e.g., when driving, when walking up or down stairs, when carrying heavy or fragile items, when playing sports or in a musical group).
- Ask students to name a few examples in their lives when they were distracted.
- Ask these follow-up questions:
  - "How long did it take you to get back into focus?"
  - "How easy is it to get distracted? In school? At home?"
  - "What were some ways that worked in getting you to focus again?"
  - "Is it always a bad thing to be distracted?"

Step 3. Students create a chart to monitor their behaviors.
- On the top of a blank page write the title question as "At this moment, am I doing my work?"
- Below that question, divide the page by drawing a line down the center.

- The left side will be the date and the time column.
- The right side will be the Focus column, where students will answer if they are doing their work with either a "yes" or a "no."
- Students can start with their first entry by writing the date and time. They all can start out with a yes!

Step 4. Tell students how to use the chart.

- From now on, students can use this chart on their own to check on their own behavior and monitor if they are on task or not. It can be used in any class.
- Tell students to add a note next to the entry whenever they choose "no," explaining the distractions that led them to go off task.
- Note: You can decide how often you want students to use this chart!

Step 5. Make a plan for periodic check-ins.

Let students know when to use this chart and when you will follow up with them. As a follow-up, use this chart as a tool to keep students focused in all classes and refer to the chart as much as possible. You may ask students if they notice any specific distractions or certain days or times they need the most time to refocus. These distractions can also be reviewed when students are referred for discipline violations within the school.

Self-Regulation in Math

The term "high -stakes testing" can send a clear message to students about the importance of their performance. While self-regulatory challenges can occur in any academic situation, anxiety around mathematics learning has a particularly robust research literature. Researchers (e.g., Foley et al., 2017) describe a vicious cycle of math anxiety and poor achievement: as anxiety grows, performance suffers; as performance suffers, anxiety grows.

Rozek, Ramirez, Fine, & Beilock (2019) describe an intervention meant to address test anxiety in STEM classes. These authors describe the way that anxiety can interfere with positive academic outcomes, positing two pathways: distracting anxious thoughts and, relatedly, physiological arousal. To meet these two challenges, the authors implemented a two-pronged intervention, using both expressive writing and cognitive reappraisal prior to exams. In this process, they:

- Ask students to "write about and express their thoughts and concerns" (Rozek et al., 2019, p. 1554). As these authors explain, this "can aid emotion regulation and perceived control of stressful situations, thereby 'offloading' worries and freeing cognitive resources that can be used to optimize performance" (Rozek et al., 2019, p. 1554).

- Help students reappraise the anxiety and understand that it can be motivating if channeled in a positive way (we'd add that Keep Calm can help with this!). "That is, rather than a sign of anxiety or failure, physiological arousal (e.g., a racing pulse) can be viewed as a beneficial and energizing force" (Rozek et al., 2019, p. 1554).

An additional illustration can be drawn from the authors' work with a high school math teacher in a private school. This teacher noted that (a) she often asks students to work in pairs to solve challenging math problems; and (b) math is a particularly stressful subject area for many of her students. Both of these challenges can be framed in terms of self-regulation. The social nature of paired or group work can often lead students "off topic" and excessive stress, as noted above, can impede focus. And she recognized the intense academic stress experienced by many of her students throughout the day, let alone in math class. The school had been implementing a character education initiative based around a set of values and the math teacher decided to become more intentional about linking her efforts with those going on throughout the school. She interspersed the language of the school's central values into the regular flow of her class, taking a few minutes to discuss with the students how they understand and enact these values. Students were asked to be intentional about these values in their interactions in their paired/group work. She added check-ins for students to share how particular values played out in their work in her class and in their lives more generally.

It became evident that these forays into values were not seen by students as a "time out" from regular class work to focus on "fluff." Rather, they were appreciated as an enhancement of learning, and they augmented, rather than impeded, work with the rest of the curriculum. In a brief feedback survey (in order to promote maximal freedom of expression, this was administered by an outside researcher, and was conducted anonymously and after grades were due), findings indicated that students strongly supported this work and saw that it enhanced their learning in the class. The students are in a setting with high academic expectations, and math can be an anxiety-provoking topic. Students described the values-based discussions as being "stress relieving." Brain-based educational recommendations often include the advice to focus on shorter educational units, with more breaks in between. Similarly, students appreciated that the sessions "gave us a break and brought variety to the class and made class more exciting." Students also saw their paired/group work running more smoothly, with one student even reporting that the values and self-regulation techniques she learned helped her manage a situation in which she "was doing a group project in physics and one of my group members was slacking off a little bit."

Physical Education and Sports

With childhood obesity and its associated health risks on the rise, physical education has taken an increasingly important role in schools. In our experience, physical education teachers are particularly quick to "get" the skill-building approach described in Chapter 2. They resonate with a holistic approach that encompasses action, emotion, and thinking. They understand that complex actions need to be broken down into smaller components and that there is no rushing that process.

Physical education also poses unique challenges with regard to self-regulation. In these classes, behavior management can be particularly difficult; they "are a prime location for the occurrence of behavior problems because of a typically less structured and more open environment" (White & Bailey, 1990, p. 353). Those less skilled at an activity can raise the frustration levels for both themselves and their peers. Even for those who may excel, there can still be frustrations involved in learning and mastering new skills (Kolovelonis, Goudas, & Dermitzaki, 2011).

At the same time, physical education provides distinctive opportunities to address self-regulation in a venue that is particularly motivating for some students. Despite the ubiquity of highlight reels featuring individual feats of athletic prowess, success in sports—both team and individual—often takes as much self-control as it does self-exertion. To hold off on swinging at a pitch outside of the strike zone, or to try for a strategic base hit and not swing for the fences. To pass rather than shoot. To conserve one's energy by not trying for the all-but-impossible play that requires sprinting across court. When one plays on a team, cooperation and patience are needed, along with respect for a variety of strengths and limitations.

Keep Calm at the Foul Line

When all eyes are on us at a crucial moment, the stress can seriously impede performance. Even professional athletes "choke" under pressure. A physical education teacher can use high-pressure situations as opportunities to build self-regulation. One creative educator we worked with used video clips of basketball stars (at the time, mostly featuring Michael Jordan) to make his point. What does this player do as he or she lines up for a foul shot? Takes a deep breath or two and focuses. Wow... LeBron James just used Keep Calm! So do baseball players entering the batter's box and tennis players before a big serve. If Keep Calm works for Mike Trout or Serena Williams, it can certainly work for our 6th graders! Physical education provides many opportunities to practice Keep Calm in "real" situations.

Constructive Reflection

Above, we described an example of a math teacher asking her students to reflect on how they functioned as a work-partner or member of a team. Reflection of this sort can become a part of physical education class as well, asking students to move beyond "How'd I do?" as an individual player, to think of one's self as a member of a team. How did I support the play of others? When did I step up appropriately? When did I share the action? How did I—or could I—keep teamwork in mind as I play? What distracts me?

Self-Regulation for Educators

The importance of self-regulation for educators is underscored by Jennings and Greenberg (2009), commenting on the results of their research. Challenges in self-regulation can become part of a cascade of negative classroom outcomes. This can lead teachers to

> face situations that provoke emotions they have difficulty managing, their classroom management efforts lack effectiveness, the classroom climate is suboptimal, and they may experience emotional exhaustion provoking a "burnout cascade." They may develop a callous, cynical attitude toward students, parents, and colleagues (depersonalization) and eventually grow to feel they are ineffective teachers (lack of personal accomplishment). Teachers who experience burnout are less likely to demonstrate sympathy and caring to their students, have less tolerance for disruptive behavior, and are less dedicated to their work (Farber & Miller, 1981).
>
> (Jennings & Greenberg, 2009, p. 498)

However, there is evidence that many teachers lack confidence in their abilities to self-regulate and, therefore, are less likely to try to do so (Sutton, Mudrey-Camino, & Knight, 2009). Some suggestions related to self-regulation are included here:

Staying in Community-Enhancing Mode While Under Stress (or, How Can I Promote SECD When All I Want to Do Is Scream!?)

We've all been there. A student says or does something in just the sort of way that pushes your buttons. Perhaps it comes while you are distracted by some other professional or personal stress. Or, perhaps it happens when all is going smoothly, and serves to derail an otherwise wonderful day. Whatever it is, it puts us at risk of reacting in a way that would, to say the least, not model excellent SECD behavior. It has the potential to undermine hard-won efforts at community building. Here are some SECD-friendly tips.

1. Identify what pushes your buttons
    We each react differently to similar situations. One person may thrive in a classroom full of loud debate among students, while another might see this as grounds for panic. Or, perhaps your at-risk situations have less to do with the students and more to do with general life circumstances, such as running late because of a tie-up on the expressway on

the way to work, or an argument with a spouse or child on the way out of the house. Knowing what pushes your buttons can help you know when to be extra careful about how you react.

2. Maintain a positive, problem-solving mindset

Easier said than done, of course, but we have found it helpful to recall the 24-Karat Golden Rule of Education: *"Do unto your students as you would have other people do unto your own children."* Empathize with the other person's situation, even if you disagree.

3. Practice a technique for de-escalation

Deep breathing? Counting to 10? Visualizing your happy place? Whatever your technique, identify it and practice it, even in situations of minor stress. Also, remind yourself to use your BEST social skills (Chapter 7) in handling relationships. This acronym, which stands for Body posture, Eye contact, Saying the right words (Skipping the wrong words), Tone of voice, helps us convey that we respect people and want to be with them.

4. Let your challenges help your students learn

Discuss with students the challenges of keeping calm and focused under stress, and the strategies you use to do so.

Communication and Relationship Skills

Background

Picture your worst classroom experiences, either as a student or as a teacher. Very likely, you did not feel adequately heard. Perhaps there was lack of clarity in expected procedures. The tone of voice being used could have been off-putting. Most telling is that you did not feel a sense of closeness and connection, a feeling of mutual respect and comfort during your times in that classroom, or at least during many of them. Now, contrast this with your best classroom experiences. The comparisons are obvious.

Recognizing this, it should be no surprise that communication and relationship skills feature prominently in the CASEL 5 competency SEL framework. These are basic aspects of life—relevant as mother and child communicate immediately after birth and thereby set their relationship in motion. Of course, many things will determine the course of that relationship, but in this example, we can see great insight into how relationships are carried and forged by communication. Our deepest internal feelings of caring and love, if not communicated appropriately (including age and cultural appropriateness) will not become part of our relationship with others. If we do not communicate to our students that we care about them deeply, or if they are unable to accurately perceive our communications to them, we will have a classroom closer to the worst experiences of our recollection, rather than the best.

One of us did a workshop with parents, featuring an activity called "Kids Only Know What You Show." Parents were asked to reflect on the extent to which they showed various feelings to their children, including love, pride, exasperation, disappointment, anger, enjoyment. Then, they were asked to reflect on the extent to which they *felt* the same various feelings, with regard to their children. Most were shocked to realize that they expressed negative feelings more often than they realized, and out of proportion to the positive feelings they held for their children.

Their insight was that children were more likely to infer how parents felt by their communications, rather than their internal emotions or true intentions. In an era when our lives are so hectic, schedules are so demanding, and the competition for our time and attention is great, it is no wonder that parental impatience, exasperation, frustration, and anxiety will gain disproportionate expression.

For teachers, the situation is not much different. Time demands and pressures to meet various objectives can lead us to become impatient or frustrated with students and to express this more often than we realize. In our desire for them to learn, we can see the negative implications of their failure to focus, or work hard, much more clearly than they can. Sometimes, the urgency we feel gets communicated more regularly and strongly than our caring.

But there is another issue.

Most of the time—the vast majority of the time, actually—we tend to assume that what you show is what you know. We don't assume that someone who doesn't sing, never swims, avoids giving speeches, and almost never works effectively in groups and on teams really can do all of these things. We don't assume that children who act selfishly, shirk responsibilities, and bully and fight are generous, responsible and kind. Of course, these assumptions may be wrong. Sad to say, but true, our biases toward certain others may make it more or less likely that we will give them the benefit of the doubt. What's the upshot? Our ability to communicate is not only at the heart of our relationships, it's also essential for students' success. Especially for youth of color, and even more so for those affected by the multiple and ongoing trauma of poverty, any shortcomings are far less likely to be attributed to poor communication and relationship skills than to some deep and pervasive deficit. So, we must devote time to building up these competencies.

Children brought up on cell phones and social media often lack skills needed to build positive relationships and to communicate carefully and accurately to those around them, adults as well as peers. Certainly, their skills in this area will influence other SEL skills, such as perception of others' and their own feelings. However, there are some skills particular to communication and relationship building that deserve attention, and we will provide that in this chapter.

There are many skills that fall into these categories, too many to cover in this book. Here, we focus on the importance of communications skills in building relationships under an array of different conditions.

It is important to note that the vast majority of children develop SEL skills sequentially but not according to a strict timeline. That said, having a sense of grade-band expectations for where a child is likely to be with regard to communication and relationship skills can be helpful. Table 7.1 contains developmental guidelines that most educators can see in their everyday interactions with students:

Table 7.1 Developmental Expectations for Cooperation and Conflict Resolution

	Establish and Maintain Cooperative Relationships	Resolve Interpersonal Conflict
K-2	Works well in groups most of the time; has friends they interact with regularly in their grade level; is willing to include others in group activities.	Usually does not resort to violence when in a conflict with others; attempts to stay calm and talk through conflicts.
3–5	Can work well with others in groups most of the time, and usually responds well when prompted to work better with others (works through conflict and stays on-task in group settings); interacts well with at least some friends in own grade and other grades; can describe characteristics of a friend.	Does not use violence or other forms of aggression when in a conflict with others; able to talk through situations verbally without blaming; seeks help from adults when in difficulty; is assertive when confronted by others at least some of the time. May sometimes follow along or not protest when peers bully, harass, or tease peers but will express regret when spoken to about it afterwards.
6–8	Has at least one stable, positive friendship in the school; has a positive relationship with at least one adult; shares responsibility in group settings (participates in group activity and listens to others' opinions).	Uses I-messages in resolving conflict; does not use violent strategies; avoids repeatedly being in situations that lead to conflict; can remove him/herself from conflict situations; usually is assertive when confronted by others; does not participate when observing bullying and related behaviors by others.

Source: Adapted from Elias et al. 1997

Setting the Stage for Positive Communication and Relationships

Bear, Mantz, and Harris (2019) have done extensive work looking at the implications of peer relationships in classrooms. They point out what every teacher knows: when students have difficulties relating to classmates, it negatively impacts the class and can even affect the entire school. They cite the research showing, consistently, that those students who lack acceptance and support from peers are at greater risk than their more connected peers for many negative outcomes, including lower academic achievement, aggression, bullying and victimization, anxiety, depression, and poor self-concept. In their analysis, solutions lie at two levels: context and students. With regard to context, they point to intervention strategies that promote stronger and more positive peer relationships and cohesion in classrooms; with regard to the student level, they note that some students will need effective skill-building experiences to help them more successfully participate in and contribute to the relationship-building opportunities available to them in their environment.

Bear et al. make the following suggestions to teachers with regard to how to set up the classroom for successful, positive relationships:

1. Set and clearly communicate norms that support prosocial behavior and academic engagement, oppose antisocial behavior, and lead students to believe that others do care about them. Involve students in co-constructing these norms and post them visibly and refer to them explicitly.

2. Use an authoritative approach, which means explaining clearly your reasons for taking any disciplinary-related actions or behavioral interventions. This approach communicates caring and firmness to students, an important combination for building a positive and effective classroom environment. An authoritarian approach to classroom management and school discipline, which is characterized by an emphasis on strict rules and use of punitive techniques, tends to breed mistrust and anxiety in students. These interfere with both relationship building and academic learning. The authoritative approach emphasizes a balanced combination of emotional support and requirements. Emotional support is perhaps the strongest influence on positive classroom relationships.

    a. Consistently communicate expectations about mutual respect and responsibility and their applicability inside and outside the classroom, and during every part of the school day, including extracurriculars, arrival and departure, even on the bus.

    b. Highlight examples you see of positive peer relationships and encourage students to praise and support one another for prosocial behavior, such as by having students post praise notes weekly for every student.

    c. Find ways to share the strengths, interests, hobbies, skills, and talents of all students.

    d. Use seating generally and around specific projects and tasks to foster diverse interactions, including placing some students in situations that will challenge/assist the growth of their relational and communication skills.

The Responsive Classroom (www.responsiveclassroom.org/) also offers a wealth of recommendations. This approach places great emphasis on relationships, and relationships are mediated by communication. Many of the techniques they recommend can be used by students in the context of group work, as both leaders and facilitative team members, and by teachers and school support professionals in leading groups of students.

Reinforce Progress and Effort

Children at any age and at every level of ability benefit from feedback about when they are doing well and when they are improving. Notice successes, large and small, in routine activities and tasks, as well as in particular subject areas. Notice also improvements in interpersonal relationships. Let students know as a group and individually through private conversations and personal notes.

Encourage Respectful Disagreement

Being part of a well-functioning group or team means being able to disagree in a respectful way. Group members/teammates/classmates need to be instructed on the importance of disagreeing and how to do it in a proper way. Using BEST, described below, as a guideline can be helpful. When feelings are strong and disagreement may be hard to express respectfully, the use of a Disagreement Box into which concerns can be placed for later follow-up can be helpful.

Defusing Defiance

Not all disagreements can be managed easily, even with training and procedures in place. When members of groups care about what they are doing, and disagree deeply, reactions might escalate into defiance. In such situations, a group leader (whether adult or student) should take care to:

- Speak in a calm manner.
- Keep comments short—no lectures.
- Remind the upset person about rules for disagreement and rules for engagement—going to a safe and calm space—if de-escalation is difficult.
- Use BEST posture, tone, and eye contact (as described below)—avoid being directly confrontative.
- Use I-messages.
- Try to redirect or defer; do not negotiate or give open-ended choices
- Be prepared to breathe deeply, disengage, and let the group know that this will be continued later when everyone involved can speak calmly.

Reflective Endings

Having a closing ritual to end the day is a powerful form of communication and respect. It reaffirms the integrity of a class/team/group and their ongoing relationships. Among the activities that can be part of a reflective ending are shout-outs about kind, caring, helpful actions experienced during the day; one or more takeaways from the school day from classes;

something unexpected that happened; things being positively anticipated the next school day; or a calming breathing or vision or listening to a chime before moving toward dismissal.

A General Strategy for Building Communication Skills: Use Your BEST Communication Skills

BEST is an acronym referring to a basic set of communication skills relevant across cultures:

B is for Body Posture
E is for Eye Contact
S is for Speech (use appropriate words)
T is for Tone of Voice

(Adapted from Bruene Butler, Romasz-McDonald, & Elias, 2011; Elias & Bruene Butler, 2005c, 2005b, 2005a)

As an example, in different situations, a different tone of voice may be appropriate, and this may further vary by culture. However, what does not vary is the importance of tone of voice for successful, clear communication. The same is true for Body Posture, Eye Contact, and Speech.

The following lesson shows how to introduce and practice BEST skills with a K-3 population. It is followed by applications of BEST for older students. In all cases, you should modify to respect cultural norms and expectations that might apply.

Objectives

• To introduce the BEST concept
• To model and provide an overview of assertive, respectful BEST behaviors as shown by body posture, eye contact, spoken words, and tone of voice
• To begin to teach children to distinguish between BEST assertive behaviors and behavior that is aggressive or passive
• To provide children with opportunities to practice BEST behaviors in simple interactions such as offering greetings and saying goodbye

Materials

• Whole-class display of Be Your BEST
• Optional: Whole-class display of Be Your Best Grid (Table 7.2 is an example format you can use to create your own grid)
• Prepare a series of photographs and/or short clips of characters from Sesame Street, Dora the Explorer, Walt Disney films, the Arthur/PBS

Table 7.2 Be Your BEST Grid

	Too Much	*Too Little*	*BEST*
Body Posture			
Eye Contact			
Speech			
Tone of Voice			

Kids website, and other sources depicting good communication skills (appropriate body posture, eye contact, speech with nice words and in a good tone of voice), along with some clips that illustrate aggressive or passive body posture, eye contact, speech, or tone of voice. Use these during step 7 of the instructional activities in this topic.

Instructional Activities

1. Introduce the new skill of Be Your BEST.
   a. Explain that everyone will learn a powerful new skill that will help treat each other with respect. Say: "A team is successful when all members are their BEST and feel respected—when everyone on the team has a right to say what he or she thinks and feels. It is important to know how to tell people what you think and feel in a way that shows respect."
   b. Point to each letter and illustration on the whole-class display of Be Your BEST and explain. Demonstrate the concept as you point out each step (for example, stand tall with shoulders back and arms relaxed at your side to demonstrate body posture). Say: **B** is for Body Posture; **E** is for Eye Contact; **S** is for Speech (use nice words); **T** is for Tone of Voice. There are three different ways to act when you are with other people. In any situation you can be "Too Much," "Too Little," or you can Be Your BEST.
2. Describe and model *Too Much* behavior.
   a. If possible, hold up a puppet or illustration to represent Too Much. Say: "Too Much is when someone is very pushy, bossy, loud, and sometimes mean when they express how they think and feel. Too Much does not care about what others think or feel and is usually not a good listener."
   b. Model the BEST components of Too Much as you point to each letter and symbol on the BEST display. **B**: Body Posture—tense, tightened muscles; stiff back; towering over others, stomping foot; making a fist; **E**: Eye Contact—glaring; piercing stare; **S**: Speech—threats, insults, putdowns, angry words, bossiness (provide examples as appropriate

for your group; for example, stupid; dummy; you are a jerk; no, you cannot play!); **T:** Tone of Voice—harsh, loud, clipped, yelling.

   c. Ask students, "How does Too Much behavior make you feel?"

3. Describe and model *Too Little* behavior.

   a. Say: "The Too Little way of behaving is very meek and shy and lets other people have their way. Too Little is good at respecting other people's right to say what they think and feel, but they do not make sure their own rights are recognized."

   b. Display a puppet or an illustration to represent Too Little and model and describe the BEST components. **B:** Body Posture—slouched, rounded shoulders, head down, shuffling feet, tense body; **E:** Eye Contact—looking down, looking away, making eye contact briefly and then darting the eyes away; **S:** Speech—vague, indirect words (I don't know; well, sort of; maybe [mumble]); **T:** Tone of Voice—low, hesitant, squeaky.

   c. Ask students, "How does Too Little behavior make you feel?"

4. Describe and model respectful BEST behavior.

   a. Say: "When people use their BEST behavior, they say what they think and feel in a way that respects the rights of the people who are listening. When we are being our BEST, we also listen to how other people think and feel."

   b. Describe and model components of Be Your BEST: **B:** Body Posture—Stand or sit tall. Do not slump; **E:** Eye Contact—Look the person in the eye in a friendly way; **S:** Speech—Say what you see and feel. Use nice words. Do not use bad or insulting words; **T:** Tone of Voice—Use a calm and even tone of voice.

   c. Let children know that you are going to show them how to use Be Your BEST to say hello. Then demonstrate what BEST would look like when greeting someone: **B:** Body posture—Walk tall, with a slight bounce in your step. Pause as you approach the other person to make authentic contact. Face the other person; maintain a relaxed stance. Don't slump. Keep a friendly look on your face; **E:** Eye Contact—Look at the other person, with a friendly and happy look in your eyes; **S:** Speech—Use nice, polite words; for example, say, "Good morning. How are you today?" (Modify your words according to local language and norms); **T:** Tone of Voice—Use a calm, even tone of voice.

5. Practice BEST.

   a. After providing a concrete model of BEST behavior, allow children an opportunity to practice and imitate the model. Depending on the maturity of the group, a combination of the following strategies can be used:

      i. Have students stand in a circle. Select two students with good conversation skills to model how they would greet each other in the morning. Ask students whether the role players used BEST. What did they observe?

    ii. Provide students with an opportunity to practice what they observed. This can be done, for example, by going around the circle letting students practice, one at a time, receiving a greeting from the student to their right, then turning to greet the student on their left. If the group is mature enough, students can also pair up and practice.

6. Provide opportunities for repeated practice based on performance feedback.

    a. Praise students for specific behaviors that match BEST criteria and give them positive, corrective prompts for aspects missed during their behavioral rehearsal. Skills develop through practice with feedback, and improvement requires repeated practice based on that feedback. Multiple practice opportunities are needed for skills to develop. You can promote development of the skills by offering coaching, much like that provided by the director of a play, both in this lesson and in the course of other daily activities.

    b. Ask students: "What parts of BEST did you use? Can you think of a way to make your BEST even better?" Providing students with concrete feedback is helpful.

    c. Examples include:

        i. "You did a great job of saying nice words. I wonder if you could use a little bit louder tone of voice? Try it again and see if that makes your BEST even better."

        ii. "Your tone of voice was great and you used nice words, too. Your BEST could be even better if you try again and remember to make eye contact when you say hello. Try it one more time and remember to look him in the eye."

7. Practice identifying BEST behavior components.

    a. Show students photos or video clips (prepared ahead of time) illustrating characters communicating using BEST behaviors. Ask students to describe what they observe about body posture, eye contact, speech and words used, and tone of voice.

    b. As behaviors are described, ask students to give a thumbs up if it is BEST behavior, or a thumbs down if it is Too Much or Too Little behavior. For Too Much or Too Little behaviors, ask students whether they can think of a way that the characters could change their behavior to be their BEST.

    c. Ask students to role play what the BEST behavior would look like. Allow several students to suggest ways to change Too Much or Too Little behavior to BEST behavior.

8. Follow up.

    a. In-Class Assignment: Ask students to share what they learned from the lesson. Ask them to think about times when it is important to use BEST. Let children know that you will be using the word BEST as a cue or reminder when they need to change their behavior. Ask children to practice using their BEST.

   b. The following activities will give students a chance to continue working with the new concepts throughout the school day and at home.
      i. Divide the class into groups of four and let each group draw and decorate one of the letters from BEST.
      ii. Have them work as a team to illustrate what their letter means.
      iii. Display their illustrated BEST letters in the classroom as a visual prompt and reminder to Be Your BEST.
9. Promoting Transfer and Generalization of Skill
   a. Continue to use BEST coaching and skill prompts throughout the day. Encourage children to prompt each other to use their BEST skills.
   b. Look for opportunities to identify and praise specific BEST behaviors such as a nice tone of voice, good eye contact and body posture, and nice words.
   c. Using photos and illustrations that you create and gather, put together and display a Be Your BEST Grid in the classroom. Table 7.2 is a blank example for you to refer to when creating the grid. Use a poster board or another large display surface for your classroom grid.
   d. Create and put up posters illustrating BEST (and other SECD skill prompts) in the classroom and elsewhere in the school. Refer to them often to help children learn to transfer and generalize BEST skills to multiple and varied situations and settings. As students gain more practice identifying these behavioral distinctions, it will be possible to use the posters to prompt skill use.
   e. When reading stories aloud, point out characters that are using BEST behaviors.

Tips for Teachers

1. The objective of this topic is to demonstrate BEST behaviors as a way to clarify what respectful communication looks like, feels like, and sounds like. Once taught, the goal is to provide multiple and varied practice opportunities of BEST to help students develop the skills needed to meet the behavioral expectation that they treat and communicate with others respectfully.
2. The terms Too Much and Too Little behaviors have evolved over time. In some earlier work, they were referred to as Monster and Mouse—terms that have been used with younger children to help describe the distinction between aggressive and passive behavior. These terms were

borrowed from the book *The Mouse, the Monster, and Me* by Pat Palmer (1977, Impact Publishers), which is a good resource, but the content focuses on respect and responsibility rather than going into depth and detail about the behavioral distinctions. Also, Monster and Mouse seem like pejorative labels as opposed to descriptions. With this in mind, we began to use the terms Blaster and Shrinker. Now, we've shifted the terminology once again, this time due to the violent connotations of "blasting." You should feel free to substitute any terms you feel might be more illustrative and appealing to your particular students.

3. It is important to incorporate awareness and respect for cultural and ethnic differences in what might be regarded as proper BEST behavior. For example, Latino children may be less likely to make eye contact with adult males, out of respect. These differences can be made explicit by asking children whether there are times and ways that they would not want to make direct eye contact, stand tall, or use any of the other recommended behaviors based on what they have learned in their family or culture. This is a way to further clarify the concept of respect using BEST in a way that also fosters cultural competency and awareness.

4. This activity is meant as an introduction to the BEST skills, using simple social situations. The objective is to provide children with repeated behavior practice so that they can have experience and success in demonstrating BEST skills. This activity is a foundation for more emotionally challenging situations such as dealing with teasing, bullying, anger, fear, or highly frustrating situations.

5. You may want to provide some examples of respectful and not respectful behaviors and ask children to give a thumbs up or a thumbs down for BEST and not BEST behaviors. For example:
    *   Someone holds open a door for you.
    *   Someone grabs a toy out of your hands.
    *   Someone yells at you for accidentally bumping into him or her.
    *   Someone waits until your turn to speak is over before he or she starts talking.
    *   Someone calls you a name.

6. BEST introduces children to a powerful prompt that incorporates key target behaviors of many social skills programs (posture, eye contact, avoidance of inappropriate language, and maintaining a pleasant tone of voice). In reviewing discipline data in many of the districts we work with, we have noted that student disciplinary action is often the result of provoking other students or adults through insults, a challenging tone of voice, aggressive body posture, glaring eye contact, or whining that sets off reactions from other group members. Improved BEST behavior thus becomes a form of anti-provocation training.

Be Your Best: Academic Connections

BEST can be integrated into many different academic situations and content:

1. BEST can be used in Language Arts to help students look at how authors portray characters. In picture books in early grades, teachers can alert students to look at the body posture and eye contact of characters, as well as to note how artists communicate tones of voice. As students develop reading skills, they can look at how authors use BEST differently for different characters.
2. Whenever students have to make presentations, formally or informally, they can use BEST to practice and make their communication as effective as possible. Box 7.1 is a BEST Communication Rubric that can be used by peers to help one another practice for and prepare for presentations.
3. When students are working in groups, they can be reminded to use their BEST behavior to work together effectively.
4. During conflict resolution, restorative circles, or any discipline-related situation, students can be reminded and prompted to use BEST when speaking with peers or adults.

Box 7.1. BEST Communication Rubric

Use this rubric to help students learn about BEST and then constructively give one another feedback on how well they were able to communicate their ideas/work in different situations. This can be used in any subject area, including Physical Education and other specials.

How would you rate your partner's readiness to communicate his or her ideas/work on a 1–3 scale?

1 = not quite ready to present
2 = ready with a little more practice
3 = fully prepared to present to others

Partner's Name: _____

Your Name: _____

BEST Categories	Rating (1–3)	Notes
Body Posture		
Eye Contact		
Spoken Words		
Tone of Voice		

Building Healthy Relationships

All of the SECD-enhancing, community-building activities in this book set the stage for developing positive, healthy relationships. We also recommend addressing this issue directly, as in the activity below. (Adapted from Bruene Butler, Romasz- McDonald, & Elias, 2011; Elias & Bruene Butler, 2005c, 2005b, 2005a and the MOSAIC Curriculum, www.secdlab.org/MOSAIC.)

Objectives

Students will be able to identify and describe healthy relationships.

Materials

- Student reflective journals

Instructional Activities

1. Introduce the Theme
   - Make sure that students understand the meaning of "relationship."
   - Clarify that **relationship** refers not only to romantic relationships, but also to any connection with a friend, family member, or adult in their lives.
   - Solicit students' opinions about what it means to build a healthy relationship.
   - Ask students to think about how relationships will impact their future life, college, and career goals.
2. Introduce Free-Write Journal Entry
   - Explain that a free-write means students will write about one topic until they are told to stop.
   - Explain that the students will be asked to share their writing with each other, so the students should respect privacy of other students and should not share details they are uncomfortable sharing.
   - Provide the writing prompt: "Describe what you think makes a good friendship. How do you build a good friendship? How do you try to be a good friend?"
   - Tell students to respond to the prompt in their reflective journals for 5–10 minutes.
3. Reflect on Free-Write with Pair Share
   - Assign each student a partner.
   - Tell the students to trade journals with their partners and read each other's response.
   - Ask students to compare their responses, looking for at least one similarity and one difference between the free-write entries.
   - Have some students share some similarities and differences between the entries.

- Summarize the similarities that students found and point out any differences in opinion about how to build a friendship.
- Highlight the values and/or skills that students include in their responses.

4. Conversation #1: Building Healthy Relationships
   - Use the discussion questions below to have students answer in pairs, small groups, dividing the class in half, as a whole class, for the varied question as you wish.

Discussion Questions
- How do you build a new friendship?
- What are the difficulties in making new friends?
- How do you keep a friendship?
- What kinds of problems come up in friendships?
- How do you try to be a good friend?
- How did you learn what makes a good friend? Did someone teach you?
- Was there a time when it was hard to be a good friend? How did you overcome that?
- When is it hard to be a good friend?

5. Conversation #2: Comparing Healthy and Unhealthy Relationships
   - After students have explored healthy friendships, ask them to consider what makes a relationship unhealthy. Use the discussion questions below to have students answer in pairs, small groups, dividing the class in half, as a whole class, for the varied question as you wish.

Discussion Questions
- What makes a relationship unhealthy?
- What are the differences between healthy and unhealthy relationships?
- Describe a 100% unhealthy relationship. Then describe a 70% unhealthy relationship. What is the difference?
- Why do you think students might have unhealthy relationships with friends, family, or others?
- What can you do when you think you have an unhealthy relationship with someone?

Follow Up and Academic Connections

- Help students pay attention to the relationships they choose to build—as appropriate, ask them about the positive or negative aspects of their friendships/peer relationships.
- The concept of healthy relationships and friendships connects to many classroom and school processes and content areas:
- All literature revolves around relationships and friendships. Having students describe the nature of relationships and friendships and distinguish

between good/helpful/healthy ones and bad/harmful/unhealthy ones can begin in early elementary grades and continue into high school.

- Events in history/social studies and current events also involve relationships between people and groups. This can be used as a frame for analysis.
- Within a classroom, and in various classes, students make friendships that are healthy and unhealthy. After the concepts are introduced, they can be reinforced as needed by helping students reflect on the nature of their relationships.
- Most health education curricula address relationships, either among peers or within families. These conversations can be aligned with what is being presented in those contexts.
- Art often depicts relationships and discussions of these depictions can be linked to conversations about healthy and unhealthy relationships and what they look like. This also can be connected to nonverbal communication patterns.
- Counselors, school psychologists, social workers, and others working with students having discipline difficulties will often find these students to have problematic relationships and friendships. Using these familiar concepts to speak about these circumstances can be reinforcing.

Maintaining Healthy Relationships: Communication via I-Messages

In order for sustain positive relationships, students need to be able to successfully navigate disagreement. Communicating around conflict using I-Messages is one way to prevent conflicts from escalating. The following activity (adapted from Bruene Butler, Romasz- McDonald, & Elias, 2011; Elias & Bruene Butler, 2005c, 2005b, 2005a and the MOSAIC Curriculum, www.secdlab.org/MOSAIC) provides a basis for introducing and practicing this skill.

Objectives

Students will be able to provide I-Message responses to example situations.

Materials

Student Handout (Table 7.3. Types of I-Messages)

Step 1. Introduce 4 types of I-Messages
- Explain that clearly communicating what you are thinking and feeling is an important part of healthy relationships.
- Ask students if they've ever had a problem with a friend that they didn't know how to talk about.

- Introduce the concept of an I-Message by presenting the handout/chart, Types of I-Messages. Ask students to read four types of I-Messages on Table 7.3.
- Define I-Messages through a class discussion using the questions below.

Discussion Questions

- What do you think a u-Message is?

  "You are annoying."
  "You are bothering me."

- How do you feel when someone uses a u-Message to speak to you?
- Why do you think an I-Message would work better?
- U-Messages make people feel bad, so they might not listen!
- Can you think of a time you were able to use an I-Message effectively?

Step 2. Solicit Realistic Student Examples (as realistic as possible!)

- Present the detailed chart of the types and examples of I-Messages (Box 7.2). Ask a student to read the Type 1 situation. Have students work in small groups and come up with alternative ways to communicate the I-Message. Share with the full group and discuss. Repeat for the other three types.
- Encourage students to think of responses they would actually use.
- Ask students if the examples are realistic—if not, encourage them to think of their own situations and responses.

Step 3. I-Messages: Four Corners Game

- Delineate four separate corners or areas of the room to represent each of the four I-Messages.
- Read a scenario from the 4-Corners chart (Box 7.3).
- Students must quickly walk to the corner (area) for the I-Message they think will be effective.
- Have students discuss among themselves the reason they chose that type of I-Message and then create an example of what they feel will be the most effective response.
- Have each group share their response. Encourage the class to collaborate to improve messages they do not think will work.
- Continue with the other scenarios on the chart and/or make up your own examples that your class would find relevant. Or, ask students to come up with some of their own scenarios.
- Repeat!

Table 7.3 Types of I-Messages

An I-Message is a way to tell someone what you think or feel. By starting your sentence with "I" instead of "You," the other person will be more likely to hear what you have to say.

1) I Believe/Think...

- *To share beliefs/values*

2) I Need...

- *When you want someone to help you*

3) I Feel...

- *When someone is getting in the way of your needs*

4) I Don't Want To...

- *When you want to say no*

Box 7.2. I-Messages: Four Corners Game Chart

1) *For the third weekend in a row, your friend canceled on you at the last minute. You're feeling left out, sad, and lonely.*

- **Example:** *When you cancel plans, I feel upset, like you aren't thinking about my feelings.*

2) *Your mom has been spending most of her time taking care of your younger siblings instead of you. You want her to change.*

- **Example:** *I know you have a lot to do but I need to spend more time with you.*

3) *Your friend's brother in high school asked you to smoke with him, but you don't want to. Last time he asked you, you said you were feeling sick.*

- **Example:** *No thanks, I don't want to.*

4) *You told your sister to stop messing with you, and she's actually left you alone this week. You want to let her know that you noticed the change.*

- **Example:** *I like the way you listen to me. When you listen to me, it makes me feel like you care about our family.*

5) *Every time you are partners with your friend in school, you end up doing all the work. You want to let him or her know without damaging the friendship.*

- **Example:** *When you don't start working on a project at the same time as me, I feel nervous that I will have to finish everything on my own.*

Follow Up

- Encourage I-Messages to de-escalate conflict in the classroom.
- If a conflict occurs, encourage students to think about what others are thinking and feeling.

Box 7.3. Definitions for Four Corners Game

Type 1: I believe...
(or I think/like)...

Use when: *You want the person you're talking with to know about your beliefs, attitudes, or likes.*

SITUATION: One of your friends is mad at you for not coming to her house on the weekend. You told her that you have to help your mom, but she doesn't understand. She says, "You have to make more time for your friends."

EXAMPLE I-MESSAGE: "I believe family is the most important relationship, and I have to be there for them. But I will try to make more time to hang out with you after I'm done helping my family."

Type 3: I Feel

Use when: *Someone is getting in the way of your needs and you want them to know what is bothering you.*

SITUATION: You're in gym class and it's your turn to do a layup while you learn basketball skills. Right when you're about to shoot, someone yells to make you fumble in front of everyone.

EXAMPLE I-MESSAGE: "I feel disrespected when you yell and mess me up."

Type 2: I need...

Use when: *You want someone to act differently.*

SITUATION: You have been quiet for the past week, hoping your friends will ask you what is wrong. Instead it seems like they don't even notice.

EXAMPLE I-MESSAGE: "When I get quiet, I need you to ask me how I'm doing because it's hard for me to say when something is wrong."

Type 4: I Don't Want To

Use when: *You want to say no to someone.*

SITUATION: You're feeling overwhelmed with your responsibilities at home and school when your favorite teacher asks if you could run for student council president. You know that you have no time, but don't want to let down the teacher.

EXAMPLE I-MESSAGE: "I would love to do it, but I don't want to take time away from homework and taking care of my little brother."

Academic Connections

- I-Messages are a basic form of communication that can be analyzed and reflected on in a variety of academic contexts.
- In literature, as well as in communications reviewed in social studies and current events (such as speeches), students can examine the extent to which I-Messages and u-Messages are being conveyed and what the impact of these are on understanding the message and on the relationship between speaker and audience.

- Students benefit from hearing teachers model I-Messages as a complement to encouraging students to use them. Teachers also can encourage students to use them in conversation with each other, particularly during group work or projects.

Interview Preparation

For some students in upper middle school grades, their advancement will often be linked to their performance in interview situations. Some of these may be for positions within schools, for school leadership, trials for various roles, etc. Later on, these skills will be important for school entry, jobs, or college. Either way, how students communicate during interview matters.

For the activity below, have students read Steve Adubato's article (Figure 7.1) about how to interview effectively. Have them discuss it in small groups, coming up with areas they most agree with, disagree with, and questions that they would like to ask Steve if they could. Create a master list of the points of agreement, points of disagreement, and questions. Have the class discuss the questions, and perhaps consider where they might go for answers other than Steve Adubato. Then, have each student write down and keep a list of the three interview takeaways.

Think of interviews more generally, as ways people learn about one another through conversations. Being able to speak to and learn about new classmates, people who are unfamiliar/different, and people from whom you want to learn new information are situations that require good interviewing skills.

- Have students practice interviewing classmates to learn more about them and their backgrounds, and reach out to students who are isolated.
- Have students "interview" classmates who have mastered skills that others would like to improve upon. This can range from being able to tie a shoelace to math abilities to visual and performing arts talents.
- Connected to any subject area—Science, Social Studies, Art, Music, Language Arts, Health, etc.—invite practitioners into class and have students prepare for and execute interviews with them.

After any of the above interview contexts, debrief with the students and build out from Steve Adubato's framework (see Figure 7.1) to refine it for particular situations beyond the more traditional interview format for which it was mainly designed.

Communication and Relationship Skills for Educators

Educators' Communication Styles

Everyone has a communication style, and teachers' and school support professionals' communication styles influence the relationships they establish with students. Here are three helpful styles, followed by three that are less helpful:

Helpful

FRIENDLY: Take a posture of helpfulness and confidence. Show a sense of humor. Convey that you like the students.

UNDERSTANDING: Be patient. Recognize that learning comes from not knowing, and so mistakes are expected and inevitable and let students know you know this. Accept disagreement respectfully so students do not stifle their honest responses. Invite conversations outside of "normal channels" but make it clear how this should be requested by students (i.e., maintain appropriate boundaries). Be empathic in the face of student difficulties and challenges, because you have "been there."

RESPONSIBLE ADULT: Provide a structure and explain it. Create and follow a rules/norms structure for how the class/group/session will run and how people will treat one another. Emphasize fairness but make it clear that the adult decides after weighing input.

Not Helpful

ANGRY: Being accusing, sarcastic, or negative, in words, posture, or tone, puts up barriers to relationships, as well as to learning. When you lose your cool, which you will, inevitably, because you are a human being, explain and apologize.

CRITICAL: Harsh, discouraging words about students' work, or about the students themselves, create lasting barriers to connection and success. Communicating a lack of confidence in students' ability or potential robs them of motivation to learn and improve. Acting out behavior is a likely consequence of this, setting up a vicious cycle that can ruin a classroom or group.

UNCONFIDENT: When educators act unsure, change their rules and standards, do not respond clearly and decisively to student misbehavior and mistreatment, or seem distracted, this communicates to students that the adults are not in control. Paradoxically, this usually accelerates misbehavior as students try to prompt adults into setting limits and establishing healthy controls. It's easy to see how both the adult and the student communications can be misinterpreted and erode positive relationships.

How to Show Students You Are Listening

There are many steps to effective communication, including both the communicator and the receiver. A positive relationship and ongoing efforts at positive communication are reinforced when it's clear that communications

Stay on message, upbeat in interviews

Most employers, when talking to a prospective employee over the phone, decide in less than 10 seconds whether to bring the person in for a face-to-face interview.

Employers discount people for a variety of communication mistakes. Some of the biggest are mumbling or speaking so quickly the employer has to work overtime to understand what you are saying. Why would anyone call you in for an interview for a job — in which you likely will be communicating with co-workers and customers — if you can't even communicate when you are supposed to be at your best?

STEVE ADUBATO

Another mistake is conveying a lack of enthusiasm or interest about the place of employment and the prospect of working there.

These are just some of the reasons why people never get to the all-important face to face interview. If you are lucky enough to get in the door, it's how you communicate that will largely determine whether you get the job. Job interviews are pretty much the same whether you are right out of school or looking for a career change: Your goal is to communicate you are someone the organization would be fortunate to have on board.

To get an idea of the keys to coming across more effectively in an interview, I spoke with Michelle Lubaczewski, assistant director of the Career Services Employment Center at Rutgers University in New Brunswick.

What follows is my take on what Lubaczewski says are some of the keys to effective communication within an interview.

Be specific: Provide concrete examples that bespeak your experience. Don't leave out specifics, don't be vague. You lose a measure of credibility if your answers lack examples. The interviewer might wonder if you really have done what it is you claim if you fail to add depth to your answers.

Pause: Take a moment to think of the best answer. Questions can be complicated and have several parts. A lot of job candidates try to blurt out an answer. Instead, try to take one or two seconds (but not 30) to organize your thoughts so you can avoid nonsense words such as "umm," "like," "uh" and "you know."

Customize: "Cookie cutter" responses will not work. Instead, customize your response to the needs of the organization. You must connect with the employer and let get across that you know and respect them. Do your homework: Research the company to know their goals, products and other specific details you can use in responses.

Maintain momentum: Give yourself an "energy check" every few minutes to make sure you are projecting and enunciating. Many times people lose their focus, thereby losing the edge with a prospective employer.

Turn the tables: They are not only interviewing you, you are interviewing them. Find out where the interviewer is in the company, how he got there, his view of the company and what direction he thinks the company is going in. Use his answers to see if this company is a good fit for you. It is important to ask solid questions to determine whether you really want to work there. The key is to do this without being pushy, cocky, or arrogant.

Focus your message: Don't be all over the place. Determine the two or three key points you want to get across and do it while still being responsive to the questions you are asked.

Steve Adubato coaches and speaks on communication and leadership. Write to him at The Star-Ledger, 1 Star-Ledger Plaza, Newark, N.J. 07102, visit his Web site at www.stand-deliver.com or e-mail him at sadubato@aol.com.

Figure 7.1 Steve Adubato's Framework for Interview Skills

are understood. While the guidelines for good listening below are focused on adults, they easily can be adapted for, and shared with, students, for their communication with peers and with adults.

1. Orient your body toward the speaker and make appropriate eye contact.
2. Allow the speaker to finish sentences without interrupting. Listen quietly and focus on the speaker.
3. Restate what you have heard. "It sounds like…". "From what you said, it seems to me like…". When clarity is needed, start by saying what you heard, not what the other person said. "I thought I heard you say… Is that what happened? What happened before that? Who else was there?"
4. Encourage people to say more when they seem to be hesitating or have not elaborated. "I would like you to say more about that." "Can you tell me more about that, please?" "I am interested in/It would be helpful to me to hear more…".
5. Use active listening to check on the feelings being communicated. "It seems to me that you are upset about what she said. Is that right?" "I am hearing and seeing a lot of frustration in you. Is this correct? Is that what you are feeling, or is it something else, or something in addition?"
6. Try to conclude with an open-ended question to provide an opportunity for anything not said to come out. "Is there anything else you would like to say before we finish?" "Would you like to say anything else? Do you want to set a time for a follow-up conversation?" "Can you say a little more about how you are feeling/what you are thinking about what happened/what you are planning?"

Relationships and Communication in Teams

There is no doubt that workplaces are becoming increasingly team-oriented. This is true of classrooms, sports, performance groups, schools, and school faculties. So, it becomes important for students and adults to develop their ability to self-monitor and evaluate how their team is functioning, and one's own contribution to the team. From such assessments, plans for improvement can be made. Here are ten questions that you can use for this purpose, for students or for yourself and colleagues. Obviously, when team members share and compare perceptions, the most accurate picture of communication and relationships emerges.

1. To what extent do you feel your group works as a team?
2. How much do you feel you personally contribute to helping your group work as a team?
3. How much do you feel part of the team?
4. How much do you feel other members feel part of the team?
5. How often do you feel the communication in your group is clear and effective?

6. How responsible do you feel for other members' feeling as if they are part of the team?
7. How much input do you feel you have into important decisions that get made?
8. How respected do you feel in the group?
9. How much do you believe others in the group feel respected?
10. To what extent do you feel comfortable bringing up difficult topics or disagreements?

Rate response on a 5-point scale similar to this:

Not at all
To a small degree
Half the time
Mostly
Almost Always

Chapter 8

Social Problem Solving

Decisions, decisions ... so many decisions!

We make decisions when the pathway ahead is not clear. Depending on the level of emotional investment and the degree of personal and social consequence, sometimes these moments of unclarity are considered "problems." *What should I wear today?* In many cases, this is a decision made at a choice point, not in response to a problem. But problems can arise: *What if I have no clean clothes appropriate for what I need to do today (say, a job interview)? What if my clothing choices are considered "uncool" and are fodder for bullies in school?*

We make decisions all the time and the process of arriving at a decision is referred to as problem solving. Problem solving refers to putting the situation into words, examining feelings, perspectives, goals, options, consequences, making a decision about the best option to achieve one's goal, planning and anticipating obstacles, refining the decision as needed, taking appropriate action and learning from what happened to inform future problem solving. In our work, we have referred to this by different names (e.g., social problem solving, social decision making, social decision making and problem solving). Here, we refer to the wider process, and use the term, Social Problem Solving (or SPS).

When our students are faced with problems, we are often tempted to suggest (or mandate!) a solution. After all, the resolution to the problem may seem quite clear to us! While sometimes expediency will require us to step in as a solver of our students' problems, doing this regularly will do them a disservice. It is far better for a teacher to become a facilitator of a problem-solving and decision-making process, a process that the students will take increasing ownership of. After all, we want our students to be able to solve problems without us (Figure 8.1). And, we acknowledge that they will be faced with a lifetime of decisions to make and problems to solve, some of which we can't even imagine at this point. (If you grew up before the turn of the millennium it is unlikely that you could have imagined the sort of problems and decisions related to cell phones and social media that youth face today.)

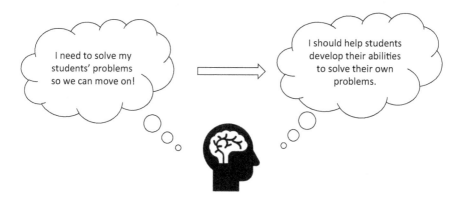

Figure 8.1 Mindset Needed for Social Problem Solving

There are a few basic understandings that inform our thinking about decision making and problem solving and how educators can become facilitators of this process.

- Problem solving is not just a cognitive activity; *emotions are integrated into the process.* Feelings appear at the start of our SPS framework (below), underscoring their importance. Emotions come into play throughout (we will have feelings related to the potential consequences of a solution, for example).
- Whether a decision or problem is "big" or "small"—or even a decision at all! —is in the eye of the beholder. For example, decisions about college may be easy to characterize as big and weighty. Yet, they are not experienced the same way by all students: Student 1: Should I go to college? If so, should I go straight from high school, or take one or more "gap" years? Which college would be best for me? Student 2: I've always wanted to go to State U. I'd be the fourth generation of my family to do so. I've been doing my best to be admitted there.
- There is *seldom just one "right" way to solve a problem,* though we sometimes jump on the first solution that comes to mind. Similarly, *even the best solutions may have negative consequences.* We strive to maximize the positives and minimize negatives; we don't wait until a "perfect" solution presents itself.
- Because of emotional hijacking (Chapter 6) we are at risk of being distracted from entering into an SPS process; *we may need to implement strategies for self-regulation before we can engage in problem solving.*
- *The problem-solving process is context dependent.* While we may use rules of thumb to shape behavior in common situations ("Always stand

up to a bully") the wisdom of any course of action is determined by one's read of the situation itself (might standing up to a violent bully put one at risk of harm; might finding an adult be a better solution in that case?).

- *Implementation matters.* A good solution "on paper" needs to be supported by consideration of the realities of putting it into play. With interpersonal problems, the communications skills discussed in the previous chapter are likely to be relevant.

The FIG TESPN Framework

In order to provide structure to the SPS process, we use an eight-component general framework acronym FIG TESPN as a mnemonic (Bruene Butler et al., 2011; Elias & Bruene, 2005b).

The FIG TESPN Framework For Social Problem Solving

F —Feelings cue me to problem solve

This first step in the process connects decision making with emotional identification and self-regulation. Once emotional hijacking kicks in, we are unlikely to engage in systematic decision making. The idea of feelings as entry points to problem solving is also discussed with regard to self-regulation (Chapter 6); without managing our emotions, we are unlikely to move ahead with the rest of this process.

I —Identify the problem

What is leading to the feeling you just identified? This seeming basic step can be deceptively complicated. The problem definition should discuss one's own experience and not focus on placing blame ("I can't concentrate with the noise in the classroom" vs "Debby's group is being too loud and disruptive").

G—Goals give me a guide

What do you want to have happen? Successful goals are phrased in a way that leaves them open to multiple solutions and are not themselves solutions in disguise ("I want to be able to work in a quiet area" vs "I want Debby and her group to shut up").

T —Think of many possible solutions

Don't settle for just one idea!! While "Debby shutting up" may be a possible solution (though one not phrased very politely), there may be options that don't involve Debbie at all! Perhaps I can ask the teacher to move farther from where the group is working.

E —Envision outcomes

For the possible solutions you generated, what might happen if you put each into effect? Make sure to include both positive and negative outcomes; there is seldom a perfect solution. Both "asking the teacher to move" and "asking Debby and her group to work more quietly" hold the potential for both positive and negative consequences.

S —Select the best solution

Based on the possible outcomes, what will you choose? Again, we are selecting the best decision, not the perfect one.

P —Plan the procedure, anticipate pitfalls, and practice

How will you put the chosen solution into action? This usually goes a long way in determining the solution's success, and often requires the use of the social and emotional skills discussed up to now in this book. If I choose to ask my peers to quiet down, how will I do so? Perhaps BEST and Keep Calm (Chapters 6 and 7 respectively) would help!

N—Notice what happened and remember it for next time

What did you learn from what you did and what might you do now? To what extent did the plan solve the problem? Are there new problems generated? Perhaps the plan didn't work out, where do things stand now?

Setting the Stage for Social Problem Solving

When promoting problem solving it is important for students to have the safety to experiment; their solutions will not always be "correct." The community-enhancing steps discussed in Chapter 3 are particularly important in this regard. There are some additional considerations about building SPS skills.

Maximize Group Work for Problem Solving

The movies *Apollo 13* and *The Martian* both depict edge-of-your-seat problem solving around real (the former) and fictional (the latter) space-age problems. While it occasionally seems that problems are solved thanks to an individual's flash of insight (*Wow, look what that guy can do with a roll of duct tape!*), if we pull back the lens, we can see that successful achievement of both missions required the active involvement of many people working in concert. The enormity of the problems went beyond one person's ability to solve them. This is increasingly becoming the case outside of the movies. As Graesser and colleagues (2018, p. 63) claim, "the complexity of problems in the 21st century are sufficiently difficult than an individual could never solve the problems alone… [T]he pressing problems of the 21st century require collaboration."

Group work in schools is commonplace. But group work does not necessarily involve collaborative problem solving. Attention must be paid to structuring the group's task so that the input of each member is needed. One way to do this is by using a technique such as Jigsaw (Figure 8.2) in which each group member first (as a member of a prior group) becomes "expert" in one element needed to complete a task. The working groups that are created to actually complete the task are then comprised of members who have gained different elements of expertise, each of whom holds a piece of the solution.

Group assignment is another element of the process in which a seemingly small intervention can have important effects on problem solving. Liljedahl (2016) highlights the benefits of *visibly randomized grouping* (randomizing the group assignments with the students observing) as compared to assigning students to previously established (either purposefully or randomly) groups.

> Students very quickly shed their anxieties about what groups they were in. They began to collaborate in earnest. After three weeks, a *porosity* developed between group boundaries as both intra- and inter-group collaboration flourished. With this heightened mobilization of knowledge came a decrease in the reliance on the teacher as the *knower* in the room. In the end, there was a marked heightening of enthusiasm and engagement for problem-solving in particular, and in mathematics class in general.
>
> (Liljedahl, 2016, p. 377)

Even seemingly minor changes can have an impact. Liljedahl, for example, found that the type of writing surfaces assigned to students working in groups to solve math problems had an impact. Groups assigned to work on whiteboard were more engaged with various elements of the process (for example, they showed more discussion and persistence). The author's explanation—that "the non-permanent nature of the whiteboards" and the "ease of erasing" allowed students to "risk more and risk sooner" (Liljedahl, 2016, p. 370)—emphasizes the social and emotional dimensions of group

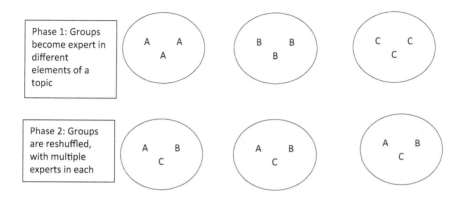

Figure 8.2 Jigsaw Grouping

problem solving. Further, vertical surfaces were more efficacious than horizontal: "sitting, even while working at a whiteboard, still gives students the opportunity to become anonymous, to hide and to not participate. Standing doesn't afford this" (Liljedahl, 2016, p. 370).

Facilitative Questioning

Teachers can introduce the language of problem solving through the questions they ask of students, as summarized in Box 8.1. Open-ended, facilitative questions can be used to scaffold students' use of FIG TESPN. It will sometimes be possible to walk a student through the entire process. At other times, you might choose one or two steps in the process to emphasize. Regardless, the main idea is to move from *telling* to *asking* whenever possible.

STUDENT: I left my textbook at home.

TEACHER [TELLING]: Here, use my copy for now.

TEACHER [USING FACILITATIVE QUESTIONING, SHORT VERSION]: What is your goal? What do you want to have happen? [Waits for student reply before telling student to use her copy of the textbook.]

TEACHER [USING FACILITATIVE QUESTIONING, LONGER VERSION]: What is your goal? What do you want to have happen? [Waits for student reply.] What are two or three different ways you can think of to solve the problem? Which of those do you think would be most likely to solve the problem? Why? How are you going to put that plan into action?

As you put Facilitative Questioning and other questioning techniques (Box 8.2) into action, make sure to take the context into account. Are you so rushed that you will likely give short shrift to the process? Is the student so distressed by the problem that your first order of business would be prompting Keep Calm (Chapter 6) and not Facilitative Questioning?

Box 8.1.   Facilitative Questioning for Decision Making and
            Problem Solving

SPS Components	Examples of Facilitative Questions
F —Feelings cue me to problem solve	How are you feeling?
I —Identify the problem.	What do you think the problem is?
G—Goals give me a guide.	What do you want to have happen? What virtues are [or, how is virtue X] relevant here?
T —Think of many possible solutions.	What are some ways for you to reach your goal?
E —Envision outcomes.	If you____, what might happen? How do these outcomes match up to the value(s)...?
S —Select the best solution..	Which idea has the best chance of meeting your goal?
P —Plan the procedure, anticipate pitfalls, and practice.	What will you have to do to make this work? What might go wrong?
N—Notice what happened and remember it for next time.	How'd it go? What did you learn for next time? How did what happened relate to the virtues...?

Source: Adapted from SDM/SPS materials (Bruene Butler, Romasz-McDonald, & Elias 2011; Elias & Bruene Butler 2005c, 2005b, 2005a)

Box 8.2. Questioning Strategies for Decision Making/Problem Solving

Use open-ended questions as much as possible

- Examples: *What happened?* or *What feelings are you having?*
- Benefits of open-ended questions
    - Develops students' problem-solving skills
    - Students become more invested in the problem-solving process, so they feel more ownership of and responsibility for the solution
- Other types of questions
    - Closed-ended
        - Requires only a "yes" or "no" response
        - Examples: *Did you hit him?* Or *Are you angry?*
        - Does not allow the student to develop critical thinking or self-awareness
    - Interrogative
        - "Why" questions
        - Example: *Why did you hit him?*
        - Makes students feel defensive

- • Students are not usually aware of the reasons behind their actions
- Multiple Choice
  - • Alternative to open-ended questions for students who are immature, have cognitive limitations, or have trouble answering open-ended questions
  - • Example: *Did you hit him because he was teasing you or because of something else?*

Two Question Rule: Follow up a question with another question

- • Follow-up questioning is an essential Common Core technique that helps students clarify their own thoughts, feelings, goals, and plans.
- • Problem-Solving Example
  - • Question 1: What are you going to say when you go up to the lunch aide?
  - • Question 2: How exactly are you going to say it?
- • Academic Example
  - • Question 1: What are the ways that the body regulates temperature?
  - • Question 2: How do you know that is true?

Paraphrasing

- • Summarize students' answers to questions and reflect their thoughts back to them
- • Helps students feel understood and taken seriously
- • **Clarification:** Helps you clarify what they meant and helps them build vocabulary
- • **Translation:** Students' responses into more accurate or appropriate responses. Example: "He's an idiot" can be paraphrased as, "It sounds to me like you are really angry with him."

Source: Adapted from SDM/SPS materials (Bruene Butler, Romasz-McDonald, & Elias 2011; Elias & Bruene Butler 2005c, 2005b, 2005a)

General Strategies for Enhancing SPS

As with Facilitative Questioning, our general approach to enhancing SPS within academic content areas involves making evident a strategy and scaffolding the use of this strategy in a wide variety of situations. Such scaffolding can build students' understanding of the SPS process, increase their perceptions of their abilities and ability to see applications of the SPS process to other subjects (Atmatzidou, Demetriadis, & Nika, 2018).

Box 8.3. SPS Scaffolding Worksheet

---

1. Feelings:

2. Problem:

3. Goal

4. Think of many solutions	5. Envision consequences
a.	(+) (-)
b.	(+) (-)
c.	(+) (-)
d.	(+) (-)

6. Select the best solution:

7. Plan and be prepared for pitfalls: What plans will need to be made?

8. Notice what happened. Now what?

Source: Adapted from Naftel & Elias 1995

A generic scaffolding worksheet is included in Box 8.3. The open-ended nature of this worksheet makes it broadly applicable. Later in this chapter we'll also show adaptations that can be made for specific content areas.

Should FIG TESPN be practiced as a "whole," from start to finish? Can components be practiced in isolation? There are advantages to the former and the strategies described above are designed to walk students through all eight steps. However, this is not a mandate; there are situations in which parts may be more advantageous than the whole! Time is a constant consideration. So are student needs. Are you noticing that students need more practice with one or more of these elements? If so, then focus on those.

General Game Plan for Using the SPS Worksheet

There are countless opportunities to adapt this SPS worksheet for use in academic content (we'll talk about using it for real-life interpersonal problems later in Chapter 9). All that is needed is a presenting decision, problem or conflict. Students then use the prompts to work through the SPS process. Note that the +'s and –'s in step 5 (Envision Consequences) are included as prompts for students to list positive *and* negative consequences.

Step 1: Review the steps of FIG TESPN

Step 2: Let students know that decision making and problem solving are important to this subject area (e.g, social student, language arts, math, etc.).
- Ask students if they can think of examples of decision making and problem solving in this content area.

Step 3: Distribute the Worksheet in Box 8.3. Explain that we'll be using this to think about a problem related to what we've been learning.

Step 4: Review the content being addressed in class
- Ask students who is faced with a decision or problem?

Step 5: Ask students to work independently or in groups to think about the problem from the point of view of one of the people/parties involved.
- Alternatively, have half the students complete the worksheet from the point of view of one person or party involved in the problem, and the other half complete the worksheet from the point of view of the other person/party involved. Have the groups compare their perspectives on the problem.

What we teach is, of course, specific and not generic. What follows are some examples of decisions and problems that can be applied to various subject areas.

SPS in Academics

Social Studies

- Should the USA enter the First World War or remain neutral?
- Should a Jew in the Warsaw Ghetto join in the uprising or not?
- Should our community use an empty lot for a new park or for new houses?
- Should a colonist side with the Loyalists or the Patriots?

The following questions focusing on emigration (Elias, 2004) can be used as either an adaptation of the SPS Worksheet, or as Facilitative Questions for a class discussion.

- How did immigrants feel about leaving their countries?
- What countries are they leaving?
- What problems were going on that made them want to leave?
- What problems would leaving bring about?
- What would have been their goals in leaving or staying?
- What were their options and how did they envision the results of each possibility?
- What plans did they have to make? What kinds of things got in their way at the last minute? How did they overcome the roadblocks?
- Once they arrived, how did they feel? What problems did they encounter at the beginning? What were their first goals?

Language Arts

Use the SPS Worksheet to work through decisions and problems faced by literary characters such as:

* Charlotte the spider [in *Charlotte's Web*]
* Jess and Leslie in their various interactions with Janice, and vice versa [in *A Bridge to Terabithia*]
* Bean's various interactions with her sister [in *Ivy and Bean*]

Also, The SPS Book Analysis Worksheet (Box 8.4, based on Elias & Naftel, 1995) is adaptable for use in many situations.

For young students, consider a "SPS Book Talk":

SPS Book Talk

Step 1: Read to the class a section of a book that presents an interpersonal problem of conflict.

Step 2: Pause before you read about how the character(s) solved their problem or resolved their conflict.

Step 3: Use Facilitative Questions to lead a discussion in which students discuss the feelings of the characters, identify the problem and goals, think of different solutions, etc.

Step 4: Continue reading the book to show the solution that the characters actually put into effect.

Step 5: Again, use Facilitative Questions to process the characters' actions with the students. (What did the characters decide? How did they put their plan into action? What happened?)

SPS and Project Planning

When students need to complete an assignment, as individuals or in groups, there are many decisions to be made, and actions to be planned. Projects can be an opportunity to develop skills in SPS while learning about the topic of the assignment. The following two worksheets (Boxes 8.5 and 8.6) are designed to stimulate creative thinking about how students can go about formulating and presenting projects.

SPS and Science

At all grade levels, science students will encounter—as a whole or in its parts—the scientific method. The centrality of the scientific method is a boon to those seeking to promote decision making and problem solving. While the scientific method is distinct from the eight-step SPS model we

---

Box 8.4. SPS Book Analysis Worksheet

1. Think of an event in the section of the book assigned. What and where did it happen? Put the event into words as a problem.
2. Who were the people that were involved in the problem? What were their different feelings and points of view about the problem? Why did they feel as they did? Try to put their goals into words.
3. For each person or group of people, what are some different decisions or solutions that might help in reaching their goals?
4. For each of these ideas or options, what are all of the things that might happen next? Envision and write both short- and long-term consequences.
5. What were the final decisions? How were they made? By whom? Why? Do you agree or disagree? Why?
6. How was the solution carried out? What was the plan? What obstacles were met? How well was the problem solved? What did you read that supports your point of view?
7. Notice what happened and rethink it. What would you have chosen to do? Why?
8. What questions do you have, based on what you read? What questions would you like to be able to ask one or more of the characters/the author? Why are these questions important to you?

Simplified Version

1. I will write about this character…
2. My character's problem is…
3. How did your character get into this problem?
4. How does the character feel?
5. What does the character want to happen?
6. What questions would you like to be able to ask the character you picked, one of the other characters, or the author?

Note: It is also possible to ask students to draw the responses to all or some of these questions.

---

present, there are many parallels (Table 8.1). And, the choice points within the scientific method provide opportunities to scaffold problem-solving skills.

Increasingly, science has become a matter of common discourse, woven into discussions about politics, policies, and how we live our life every day. "Paper or plastic" was once a question of bag preference posed by the cashier in the grocery store. Now, a consumer must consider the merits of

---

Box 8.5. Planning Our Project
(From the MOSAIC Curriculum)

To show what we have learned about:
We will:
Brief description of what we plan to do:

Some Ideas for How Students Can Express Themselves:

- Doing a photo essay
- Writing a report
- Keeping a journal
- Select a song to share
- Write song lyrics or rap lyrics
- Compiling a collage
- Building a model
- Doing a statistical chart
- Recording interviews
- Setting up an experiment
- Designing a mural
- Choreographing a dance
- Making a video
- Creating a rap or a song
- Giving a PowerPoint presentation
- Developing a musical
- Writing a play or commercial

---

each choice (or the choice of "no bag" or "reusable bag") for environmental sustainability. A phone was once a one-trick pony—it made phone calls. Now, issues of privacy are pressing even when our phones are not in use.

This enmeshment of science and everyday life decisions has come to be referred to as *socioscience*. Socioscientific issues are "ill-structured", lack "a single solution or a single solution path" and "involve multiple, often conflicting, stakeholders and multiple ways to gauge the success of a solution" (Belland, Gu, Kim, & Turner, 2016, p. 1137). From a policy-making perspective, socioscientific issues can be vexing. From the standpoint of promoting SECD growth, grappling with these sorts of issues can be invaluable. In working through socioscientific issues, students must combine an understanding of science with taking the perspective of the various constituents (Chapter 5). They must think of consequences not only in terms of scientific knowledge but also "on the basis of the extent to which the solution was justified acceptably through persuasive argumentation" (Belland et al., 2016, p. 1137), calling on communication skills (Chapter 7) to augment the problem-solving process.

Box 8.6. Taming Tough Topics

(Adapted from Social Decision Making/Social Problem Solving Material)

First: Define your problem and goal

1. What is the topic?
2. What are some questions you would like to answer about the topic, or some things about the topic you would like to learn?

Second: List alternative places to look for information

1. Write at least five possible places where you can look for information

    a. ---
    b. ---
    c. ---
    d. ---
    e. ---

2. Plan which ones you will try first.
3. If these ideas do not work, whom else can you ask for ideas? Where else can you look for information?

Third: List alternative ways to present the topic

1. Write at least three ways in which to present the topic. If it is a written report, write three different ways that it can be put together.
2. Consider the consequences for each way, choose your best solution, and plan how you will do it.

Fourth: Make a final check and fix what needs fixing

1. Does your presentation answer the topic and the questions you asked? Is it clear and neat? Is the spelling correct? Will others enjoy what you have done?

Fruitful exploration can occur with a variety of topics in which science intersects with values, such as genetic testing (Sadler & Zeidler, 2004), ecology and pollution (Belland et al., 2016), and energy conservation (Levinson, 2018). As an example, educators in a middle school class in Berkeley Heights, New Jersey, used an SPS approach to thinking about environmental problems, using the scaffold in Box 8.7, an adaptation of the general worksheet in Box 8.3. An abbreviated version of what was developed is shown in Box 8.8.

Table 8.1 SPS and the Scientific Method

Component of Scientific Method	Related Facilitative Questions
Observation and problem formation	• What did you see? • What is something you want to know more about or something that you are curious about? • What is the problem that you are working on?
Collect information	• What are at least five possible places where you can look for information? • Which will you try first? How will you go about doing so? • If these ideas do not work, whom else can you ask for ideas? Where else can you look for information?
Formulate a hypothesis	• Based on the information you collected, what are some possible explanations that would resolve the problem? What is your explanation that you want to test?
Experimentation	• What are different ways in which you can test your hypothesis? • What will you need to do in order to actually conduct your experiment? • What outcome(s) would support your hypothesis? • What outcome(s) would disconfirm your hypothesis?
Data analysis	• What was the result of the experiment? • Does the result support your hypothesis?
Conclusions	• What was successful about your experiment? What might you do differently if you were to do your experiment again? • What new questions are raised by the findings of your experiment? • If the findings do not confirm your hypothesis what alternate hypothesis will you test, and how will you go about doing so?

Box 8.7. SPS Discussion of Environmental Problems

Student(s)_____ Date: _____

1. Feelings [Example: Anger, shock, fear, frustration]
2. Identify the problem: [Example: If things continue the way they are, the environment will be in terrible shape.]
3. Goal(s) [Example: To take individual responsibility and actions to help save and protect the environment.]
4. Think of solutions [Example: Anything from "Storm Washington DC" to "Teach our families to do environmentally safe things."]
5. Envision outcomes: [Example: Whatever might happen, from "It would cost too much" to "People would get angry."]
6. Select the best solution [Example: Teach our families to do environmentally safe things.]
7. Plan [Example: Share information and facts at home; practice what we will say; develop plans at home to recycle, reuse, reduce.]

Box 8.8. SPS Discussion of Environmental Problems (Example)

Student(s)_____ Date: _____

1. Feelings: Angry, frustrated
2. Identify the problem: There is no plastics recycling in our town.
3. Goal(s): Get plastics recycling in our town.
4. Think of solutions

    Go door-to-door
    Letter to mayor
    Survey
    Share information at home
    Newspaper editorial
    Booth at food store
    Protests
    Letters to president

5. Envision outcomes: [Students had discussion of pros and cons of each solution, giving consideration to time, feasibility, and resources.]
6. Select the best solution: A combination of ideas: Go door to door, visit town hall, set up a booth at the food store, and send letters to the president.
7. Plan

    Practice and plan a call to the mayor.
    Prepare for a meeting with the mayor.
    Send out surveys to gain support, plan speeches.
    Share information at home.

8. Follow up: Write letters to the newspaper.

Connection With Creativity

While creativity is not new on the educational scene, it has taken a position of increased centrality. Why? Sir Ken Robinson, an influential figure in this field, points to several factors. Today's problems exist on a major scale, and there is a growing appreciation that new ideas are needed to address them. Unpredictability is the norm and old assumptions cannot be expected to hold. "Nobody has a clue what the world's going to look like in five years, or even next year actually, and yet it's the job of education to help kids make sense of the world they're going to live in" (Azzam, 2009).

We sometimes associate creativity with the wild-haired artist flinging paint onto a canvas, or someone who sits bolt upright in bed with an "Aha" realization of a new insight. While creativity can and does take that form, it is, at essence, "a disciplined process that requires skill, knowledge, and control" (Azzam, 2009) along with imagination and inspiration. The hard work may be less visible than the creative outcome, but both the paint-flinging artist and the insightful insomniac have likely been engaged in a process that began well before their moment of insight.

Creativity is, at its root, a way of thinking and solving problems, and doing so in novel ways. Using a ladder to reach a ball stuck on a roof is an example of good problem solving. Attaching a net to a drone and using this to retrieve the wayward ball is creative problem solving. While we may think that creativity is something one "has" or "doesn't," as a way of solving problems it is something that can be cultivated. It is a process that requires both divergent and convergent thinking.

> *Divergent thinking* requires students to think of many different ideas, as opposed to *convergent thinking*, when there is only one right idea. Both are necessary for creativity: a student uses divergent thinking to generate different solutions to a problem or challenge and then uses convergent thinking to decide which one will provide the best results.
>
> (Drapeau, 2014, p. 4)

And, it is a process in which emotions are deeply relevant. I may be the most divergent of thinkers, but my creativity will be greatly diminished if I am fearful that I'll be labeled as weird for my unusual suggestions. Further, design thinking, a creative process to address problems faced by people as they navigate the world, starts from the stance of empathy. A social problem involves the experience of real people, and a social solution is only meaningful from the perspective of the person or people encountering the problem.

Many educators have noticed that students are perplexed by assignments such as "Write about whatever you'd like" or "Use whatever format you want to present your work." Students often respond by asking "But what should I write about?" or "What format should I use?" Or, they may seek validation and permission. "Can I write about my grandparents?" "Can I write about swimming?" "Can I write about unicorns?" A teacher may find herself wondering what the world record is for saying "Yes, you can write about whatever you want" in one class session. Why are students—who so value their autonomy in many cases ("Don't tell me what to do!") —at a loss in these situations? Students may have picked up on a piece of the "implicit curriculum" of schooling, those messages that are conveyed by everyday routines, and come to assume that requests posed by teachers can be done correctly or incorrectly. When faced with an open-ended task, a student may wonder about what "correct" means. *Perhaps this is some sort of test in which I need to hit upon the correct response without guidance, maybe the teacher is not being truthful and really has a right way in mind.*

The expectation that there is *a* right answer can stifle creativity and risk taking. Compounding the challenge is that in many cases it is *not* the case that all responses are correct. There may be one answer, a limited number of acceptable responses, or criteria that need to be applied. "The Day the Martians Brainwashed the President" may be a fine topic for an essay about "whatever you want to write about" but not for an essay about the causes of the Civil War.

Creating the Context for Creativity

1. Practice creative—even outlandish! —brainstorming: Brainstorming is a central component of the "T" in FIG TESPN. Students can get stuck in thinking there is only one way to solve a problem and therefore persist in trying to apply that solution even after repeatedly seeing it doesn't work. One activity that can help promote a climate of "any response is OK" involves brainstorming interpretations of ambiguous drawings. The process is simple: Draw an abstract figure on the board (some examples provided below in Figure 8.3), and ask students: "What might this be a picture of?" Accept all responses. If the students need some help, throw in an idea of your own—the more outlandish the better!! Here are some other fun exercises:
   - Brainstorm unusual uses for common objects like paper clips and rulers.
   - Work with art teachers to create art out of recycled materials.
   - Use progressive storytelling, where students go in a circle and add a creative story stem started by the teacher or a peer (e.g., Long, long ago in a land far away…; Running as fast as she could…).
   - Similarly, the class can produce a progressive drawing by taking turns adding lines or elements to a picture, without a prearranged plan.

   Note that these can be done regularly as "do nows" at the start of a class to help get creative juices flowing.

Figure 8.3 Abstract Figures for Brainstorming

2. Establish ground rules for supporting claims: While brainstorming is central to divergent problem solving, there are times in which some responses may be *too* out of the box. There may not be one correct response, and creative interpretations may be welcome, but you want student answers grounded in data. Why didn't the Tucks (of "Everlasting" fame) want the water from the farm to be sold? Responses should make sense within the context of the story; creativity needs to be grounded in facts on the ground. Here, the two-question rule can be used to good effect:

TEACHER: Why didn't the Tucks want the water from the farm to be sold?
STUDENT: They didn't want everyone living forever.
TEACHER: What parts of the story led you to that conclusion?

An interesting example is provided by Vande Zande and colleagues (2014) in the context of the Visual Arts. These educators describe using a similar problem-solving structure not only to address design challenges but also so that students learn how "to use as an effective life and career skill. Students discover through testing, revising, and retesting that there may be some solutions that work better than others but there are many possibilities for success" (Vande Zande et al., 2014, p. 20). In one example, a teacher builds on lessons about ergonomics and anthropometrics and scaffolds a problem-solving process for students to create an innovative "seating device" (the term the teacher used so that students would break out of assuming that a chair must look like a chair). A second example involved landscape design, with the students needing to design features to meet the needs of existing landscapes. In a third example, students in an Israeli pre-K program were asked to redesign airports to make them better. They worked with older students in their school whose job it was to represent their ideas in drawings and in models. The procedure built a full array of SEL skills, but was catalyzed by creativity. Skill-building continued as students prepared for, and carried out, presenting their results to parents and the community in an expo, with the younger and older kids as partners, explaining their various designs. In all cases, a problem-solving process was provided to give general guidance to the students as they proceeded.

SPS for Educators

As adults, we have had many years of experience with making decisions and solving problems. Even so, we all have room for growth. Perhaps one or more of these statements apply to you:

*   I feel like my lessons are stuck in a rut; things are going fairly well but it seems like the same old thing over and over again.
*   Things around me are changing rapidly. The kids are different these days, the mandates "from above" keep shifting. I am concerned that what I am doing won't keep working.

- I love teaching, but there is a creative side to me that I am not accessing in my work.
- Most of the students are doing just fine, but there is a subset whom I am not reaching successfully.

Having a problem-solving framework in mind can be useful for evolving one's practice. In fact, FIG TESPN shares several components with approaches to practitioner action research (PAR), a structured approach to implementing change in the classroom. In PAR, educators identify a particular problem or learning goal, plan how they will go about addressing it, put their plan into action and observe—in a structured way—the outcomes. Importantly, PAR, like FIG TESPN, is an iterative process. The process begets further opportunities to go through the process.

Looking at PAR through a lens of FIG TESPN, a teacher might consider the following questions as guidelines:

1. What are you feeling that is making you aware of a challenge or problem? Under what circumstances are you most likely to feel this way?
2. What is the problem that you are addressing? What might it be helpful to learn more about in order to better understand the nature of the problem?
3. What is your goal? What are your desired outcomes?
4. What are various ways in which you can meet your desired outcomes?
5. What are the costs and benefits of the various options?
6. Given the costs and benefits, which option is most likely to bring you closest to achieving my goals?
7. What steps will you need to take in planning a pilot project in order to test out the option that you picked?
8. How will I be proactive in making sure you can observe the results of my pilot run and learn from the experience? Now that you've tried the pilot, what are your feelings about how it went? What might you do differently next time?

Stepping back to a broader view, both PAR and FIG TESPN are part of a spirit of continuous improvement. We see the applicability of the wisdom of the Talmudic sage Rabbi Tarfon who pointed out that "It is not your responsibility to complete the work, but neither are you free to abandon it." Our growth—and that of our students—is never complete; our learning means for us to persist in what is a never-ending task.

Chapter 9

Cross-Content SECD Elements

The previous chapters addressed methods to promote competencies of emotional awareness, self-regulation, empathy, communication, relationship building, and problem solving. We recognize some fuzziness in the boundaries among these skills. Throughout, we've pointed out how the skills intersect, how success in one helps with others. Good communication, for example, will help in putting a solution to a problem into action. Like a good sports coach, though, we recognize that complex interactions can and should be broken down and practiced in their component parts. There is a certain "slow cooking" element to this, and it can sometimes get frustrating. We can all picture the aspiring player who, after seemingly endless skill drills ("Everyone run back and forth 20 times dribbling with your non-dominant hand!"), wonders when they are actually going to play basketball!

Even while practicing component parts, though, we sometimes are called to skip ahead to focus on more complicated situations. Regardless of whether the players have mastered non-dominant-hand dribbling, they have to go out and play the game scheduled tomorrow night! The parts and the whole are of course connected, and the coach could use the game as an opportunity to practice and give feedback around a particular skill. At the same time, the coach will need to look at the process more broadly, and provide input into a wide array of skills, and the combined use of these skills, whether they have been a focus or not.

Likewise, even as you focus on particular SECD competencies, situations may arise in which there are opportunities to scaffold processes that require the enactment and coordination of multiple skills, ones that have been practiced and ones that have not been.

Because the material in this chapter builds on the skills discussed previously, some of it may seem like review. In fact, at several points we will refer you back to activities that have been discussed previously. What might seem like review, though, is actually part of the process of skills transfer and generalization. A student who has practiced and improved her communication skills during content-oriented role plays cannot be assumed to now be ready to successfully put those skills into action in their own lives.

In this chapter, we discuss opportunities to build SECD in the course of regularly occurring classroom activities. We'll focus on three areas:

1. Classroom/behavior management.
2. Promoting productive focus on learning tasks.
3. Particularly productive SECD pedagogies such as service learning and group-oriented instruction.

Classroom/Behavior Management

You've established your class rules and norms (as discussed in Chapter 3) and have been incorporating SECD into content area(s). Excellent! We can make you this iron-clad guarantee: No matter how many times you reiterate classroom agreements, or how wonderful the climate of relationships in the classroom, or how many times your students have practiced all the core skills mentioned in the previous chapters … *at some point, a student will do something that is not up to expectations.* And you'll need to react to this.

There are various terms that are used to describe this element of a teacher's work, and we see each as limited: discipline (sounds heavy-handed); consequences (seems to oversimplify the matter); classroom management (too broad); and behavior management (sounds quite controlling). We'd prefer something like:

> Responding to student behavior in a way that provides opportunity to build and practice social and emotional skills.

We realize that is mighty bulky. We'll stick with the somewhat more streamlined term classroom/behavior management.

Regardless of what we call it, how can SECD help us think about how we respond to student infractions? The behaviors that we need to "manage" are usually misapplications, or non-applications, of SECD skills. Lack of self-regulation under stress. Use of an abrasive tone of voice. Not anticipating consequences. As we look to the future beyond that behavior, we think about how we can make it more likely that the student will apply the needed SECD skills.

Before discussing specific techniques, we introduce two shifts of mindset related to adopting a SECD-enhancing approach to classroom/behavior management.

Mindsets of Classroom/Behavior Management

We've already touched upon the idea of mindsets around classroom/behavior management throughout this book and in particular in our discussion of the

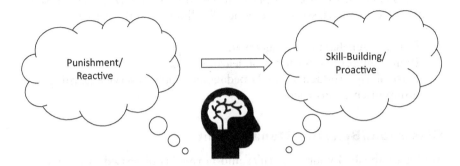

Figure 9.1 Mindset Needed for Behavior Management

language and terminology used. The bulky phrase we used reflects a mindset in which our reactions to student misbehavior are geared to helping develop the skills needed to enact the desired behavior (as opposed to, say, a punitive mindset in which an educator believes that their reaction is to cause an unpleasant experience for the student to discourage them from enacting that misbehavior again).

Our first mindset shift, then, is from *punishment* to *skill-building* (see Figure 9.1).

The ultimate goal is for students to manage their own behavior. One ramification of the skill-building mindset is that the classroom/behavior-management process requires a great deal of patience. *Why did Joey react in the same negative way, even though we dealt with it the last time it happened? Why didn't he learn?* From a skill-building perspective, the answer is clear: Skill-building takes time, and challenges in school—conflicts, for example—generally involve multiple skills. This mindset shift is related to the overall goal of an SECD approach to this topic—students should be able to "manage" (or, regulate) their own behavior, rather than having it managed by an external source.

A second shift is from a *reactive* to a *proactive stance*.

Conflict is inevitable, fights are not. Negative emotions are par for the course, "blow ups" don't need to be. An SECD-oriented approach is geared toward acknowledging that SECD challenges are a part of life, and that one needs to be ready with the needed skills and strategies to confront these. And, the best time to develop these skills and strategies is not during a crisis. *When there are conflicts in our classroom, how will we solve them?* is a question to answer (ideally, in conversation with the students) early on, not once a conflict has arisen. *What can I do if I am feeling very angry (or sad, or bored, etc.) and am having a hard time managing that feeling?* is likewise worth planning for—it will happen! —and not figuring out during a student's emotional meltdown. The language and skills that are introduced and practiced every day in class are those that will be called on in these situations.

Setting the Stage for Classroom/Behavior Management

There are likely already processes in place in your classroom that can be adapted to capitalize on their potential for building students' internal capacity to manage their own behaviors through applying SECD skills.

For example, "Tell the teacher" is an old standby used by students when problems arise. This strategy has its advantages (it brings a responsible adult into the picture to handle a potentially explosive conflict) and disadvantages (bringing a responsible adult into the picture to handle something that could have been handled *without* bringing a responsible adult into the situation). Patience is required in the latter situation. As skills develop, there will be fewer problems that require adult mediation. Meanwhile, better to err on the side of asking for help if needed.

So, the teacher has been "told." What now? This may be a great opportunity to use all or some of the Facilitative Questions introduced in Chapter 8. Assuming that no immediate crisis is looming, asking questions in these situations helps ensure that the students are an active part of solving their own problem—even with an adult having been called.

"Time Out" is another common consequence for misbehavior. We suggest applying the reactive to proactive mindset shift to thinking about Time Out. A reactive stance sees Time Out as a negative consequence to misbehavior that is supposed to make that misbehavior less likely to recur. Framed in this way, Time Out is controversial. Is this a form of teacher-mandated social exclusion? For students who don't want to be in the classroom, isn't Time Out actually a reward? In fact, there are schools in which teachers are not allowed to use Time Out. Indeed, the term has acquired so much baggage that we recommend using a term that reflects a shift from the operating principle of exclusion to that of self-management to accomplish "time in". We've included some examples below.

A proactive stance takes as a starting-off point that sometimes all of us need to get our thoughts together, to "decompress" and sit in silence, to sort out a negative emotion. In an ideal world, we'd all be able to successfully manage our emotions until we are able to get to such a quiet moment. In the real world, sometimes we need that moment *right now* or else things will spiral out of control.

Make sure the class knows the process for working through triggers and problems before they escalate, and have scaffolds at the ready. Some teachers have created a Problem Solving Zone, with the steps of FIG TESPN (Chapter 8), or any other problem-solving strategy being taught prominently featured, where students can go to engage in working out disagreements that can't quickly be resolved. Perhaps there are problem-solving worksheets that each party to the disagreement must complete. If students are experienced with FIG Footsteps (Chapter 5), this can be used as a script for perspective taking and problem solving. The Problem Solving Zone can have in it large cut-outs shaped like feet—or even pairs of over-sized slippers—that students can stand in for use in an activity such as FIG Footsteps (Chapter 5). Students would then follow the script to present their side of the problem, reflectively listen to the other side, and enter into discussion about a solution. Similar designated areas have been used for helping students to calm themselves when upset (e.g., Keep Calm Corner; Stressfree Zone; Calm Spot; Relaxation Area).

You yourself may model a quick drop-in to the Problem Solving Zone when you are at risk of a meltdown! In name of proactivity, be ready to follow up with students who seem to be accumulating Problem Solving Zone frequent flier miles. Perhaps a discussion is in order—mediated by Facilitative Questions—about the reasons the student is making frequent visits, the problems faced, the pros and cons of this approach to solving them, and possibilities for alternate solutions.

Conflict De-Escalation for Educators

Conflicts are unavoidable any place where human beings are in close proximity and/or are engaged in shared tasks and/or ongoing relationships. Conflicts reflect differences in opinion, ideas, priorities, goals, perspectives, and/or beliefs. Actions that escalate conflicts usually increase the distance between the two parties' positions; actions that de-escalate conflicts at least do not increase that distance, and at best they reduce it, or redirect focus away from the conflict at that moment.

For educators, successful conflict de-escalation begins with knowing one's own feelings, having a good understanding of the students' perspective, and the strength of the relationship with the student. Conflicts escalate when anger and other strong emotions enter interactions with students. So, how we communicate with students in conflict situations is tremendously influential on their outcomes.

General guidelines to keep in mind: one never "wins" a conflict with students by exercising one's power or ability to punish. While this may seem to end a difficult situation at the moment, it does so at the cost of the relationship you have with the student. An angry victory will take many positive interactions to undo, if ever.

Watch your verbalizations. The BEST guidelines for teaching students to communicate respectfully to one another (described in Chapter 7) apply here as well. Avoid a threatening body posture/physical stance. Physically backing off can often assist de-escalation. Make eye contact with the student but don't glare or stare in anger. Watch what you say. Avoid accusations, immediate demands, and of course any insults or negative attributions. Finally, be mindful of your tone of voice. Calmness de-escalates, as does quietness. You may not feel calm and you may want to shout, but it won't help and you won't actually feel better afterwards.

Finally, be prepared to say that you will continue the conversation later. It's especially important to not play out conflicts in front of an entire class or group, at least not any longer than necessary. It's fine to say, "I am not happy about the situation but it's best for you and I to meet [when and where] to talk this through. If you need a minute or two to get ready to [get back to whatever was going on or what is happening next], you can [specify what might be feasible]."

At the end of the day, preserving students' (and your!) self-respect and dignity is more important than the specific conflict situation you are facing. Once again, you can see how communication and relationships are so strongly connected.

Building Behavioral Reflection and Self-Monitoring

At the heart of the transition from reactive to proactive classroom/behavior management is the importance of students taking ownership over monitoring their own behaviors. A teacher waiting for something to go wrong and then providing feedback is the definition of reactive! But self-monitoring is difficult and requires—like all SECD competencies—practice under controlled conditions. A classroom practice of self-reflection—even, or especially, when this is not in response to a problem behavior—can help students develop their capacity to self-monitor their behaviors. This is even more powerful when students have a say in their goals for behavioral growth, as discussed later.

For schools that have embraced the language of virtues, we recommend the use of a reflective tool such as the Virtues Monitor (Box 9.1). For those more focused on SECD skills, the Skills Practice Worksheet (Box 9.2) achieves a similar purpose. These forms were developed as Tier 1 interventions to help students attend to the progress they are making in addressing a particular skill or virtue and are meant to be used on a regular basis.

There are some basic guidelines for using these types of tools, regardless of the particular version you choose:

1. There is great value in collaboration, with students working with buddies to help improve virtues and/or skills.
2. They can and should be used on regular basis, perhaps setting aside a few minutes at the same time each week to complete it.
3. The target virtue/skill can be the same for each student, or it can be individualized based on student needs. Any of the skills and virtues discussed to this point in the book can serve as targets.
4. They can be used as a sort of behavioral growth portfolio. You and the student (together and separately) can review progress over time. This can become the basis for discussions during parent-teacher conferences.

Box 9.1. Virtues Monitor

What virtue are you working on?

Describe a recent situation that you felt challenged your work with this virtue (what happened, where you were, etc.):

How did you feel?

How well do you think that you used the virtue in this situation?

1	2	3	4	5	6	7

Not So Great   Very Well

What is something that you liked about how you handled the situation?

What is something that you did not like about how you handled the situation?

If a similar situation happens again, how might you handle it differently? What would help you do that?

Box 9.2. Skills Practice Worksheet

Name:_____ Date:_____

Skill(s) practiced:_____

When did you do this?_____

Where were you?_____

Who else was there?_____

What did you do?_____

What did you observe?_____

How did the others react?_____

What else happened?_____

How would you rate yourself on your use of this skill?

        poor   fair   okay   good   excellent

What would you do differently next time?_____

What other skill would you like to work on?_____

Learning From Problems

So, you've done all of the above in order to proactively prevent problem behaviors and, lo and behold, problem behaviors still occur. Shocking? Not at all. But what now? Though we strongly favor preventing problem behaviors, we also recognize that there need to be consequences for these when they do occur. These Tier 2 interventions complement the Tier 1 reflective approaches to self-monitoring described above. Approaches such as Restorative Justice can integrate with SECD enhancement. For example, the worksheet below (Box 9.3; developed in a school using the Mosaic curriculum) uses the idea of "making things right" within the framework discussed throughout this book.

Box 9.3. Behavioral Reflection Sheet

Name:_____ Grade:_____ Date of Incident: _____

MOSAIC Reflection Sheet

What happened? What did I do? What was my part in the situation?

The behavioral expectations I did not follow were: *(check any that apply)*

☐ Be on time (arrival/departure/classroom)   ☐ Follow adult directions

☐ Use appropriate language   ☐ Respect others' property

☐ Be respectful/courteous/polite   ☐ Have appropriate pass

☐ Walk appropriately and quietly   ☐ Other _____

Who did my behavior harm or cause problems for? What was the harm done? What did they need from me?

Steps I can take to make things right and/or repair the harm done:

1)

2)

What did I want? What are my needs in the situation? Why did I behave this way?

☐ I wanted a student(s) attention   ☐ I wanted an adult's attention

☐ I wanted to be left alone   ☐ I wanted an object/thing

☐ I wanted to avoid doing my work   ☐ I wanted to go home/leave
the room

☐ Other _____

MOSAIC Skills that will help me get my needs met: *(check any that apply)*

☐ Communication (saying what I need, i-messages)

☐ Problem solving (working it out)

☐ Emotion regulation (calming myself down)

☐ Empathy (understanding others' points of view)

MOSAIC character traits/virtues that will help me in this situation are: *(check any that apply)*

☐ Positive Purpose   ☐ Optimistic Future-Mindedness

☐ Responsible Diligence   ☐ Constructive Creativity

☐ Helpful Generosity   ☐ Compassionate Forgiveness

☐ Compassionate Gratitude   ☐ Other _____

Positive, helpful and skillful actions I can choose next time to have my needs met are:

1)

2)

3)

Signature:_____

Date:_____

Source: Adapted from SDM/SPS MOSAIC materials

Teachers can help students reflect on what went wrong in problem situations, and plan for alternate actions if and when a similar situation happens in the future. The Reaction Tracker (Box 9.4, for younger children) and Trouble Tracker (Box 9.5, for older students) were designed to help students reflect on the social and emotional elements of problem situations.

Box 9.4. Reaction Tracker

Name:_____ Date: _____

What Happened? _____

Keep Calm	☹	😐	😊
Body Posture	☹	😐	😊
Eye Contact	☹	😐	😊
Say Nice Things	☹	😐	😊
Tone of Voice	☹	😐	😊

What did you like about what you did?

What could you have done to handle the situation better?

Source: Adapted from SDM/SPS materials (Bruene Butler, Romasz-McDonald, & Elias 2011; Elias & Bruene Butler 2005c, 2005b, 2005a)

Reflective tools such as these need to be used with the SECD basics in mind. It would be a mistake to ask students to compete these tools in the heat of an argument. Better for them to use Keep Calm first to get into a problem-solving mindset. The tool should be introduced to the class ahead of time, rather than once a problem has occurred. Ideally, students will have had experience with the FIG TESPN problem-solving framework from your work within content areas. Using reflective tools that are linked to that framework, and that refer to other SECD skills you've introduced, helps students transfer their learning to these new problem situations. These tools can be used in ways similar to those discussed for the Virtues Monitor and Skills Practice Worksheet, above. Solutions to problems can be tracked over time. Reviewing the reflections with students over time can help them discover Button Pushers, as discussed in Chapter 6 ("I notice that all of these Hassle Logs are for things that happened during recess...").

Box 9.5. Trouble Tracker

Name_____   Date: _____

1. Where were you when this happened?
2. At what time did this happen?
3. What happened?
4. What were you feeling when this happened?
5. Who else was involved?
6. What did you do?
7. What did the other person/people do?
8. How did you handle yourself?

   ☐Poorly   ☐ Not well   ☐ Okay

   ☐ Good   ☐ Great

9. How upset were you?

1 Not at all	2	3	4	5	6	7	8	9	10 Super Upset

10. What are some other things you could have done?
11. What are some things you can do now?

Source: Adapted from SDM/SPS materials (Bruene Butler, Romasz-McDonald, & Elias 2011; Elias & Bruene Butler 2005c, 2005b, 2005a)

Finally, we realize that sometimes a quick intervention is needed in the midst of a troublesome situation. The STOP procedure (Box 9.6) can be used in those situations, providing a quick script for intervention that features core SECD elements.

Promoting Productive Focus on Learning Tasks

Applying the ideas of SECD to classroom/behavior management will help create an environment in which disagreement is less likely to result in conflict and emotions can be the source of enriched experience and not of disruption. A well-managed classroom, however, does not automatically translate into a classroom in which learning occurs; successful classroom management is a necessary but not sufficient contributor to learning. A teacher must also create an environment that enhances student motivation to learn. SECD ideas and techniques can be helpful here as well.

Box 9.6. STOP Procedure

- **S   STOP AND USE KEEP CALM**
  - Say "Stop" to interrupt behavior and
  - "Keep Calm" to prompt breathing.
- **T   TAKE A LOOK**
  - Quickly Identify the <u>problem</u> - "What's going on?"
  - Then—Focus on the <u>goal</u>—"What needs to happen? What is the goal? "
- **O   OPTIONS**
  - Brainstorm ideas:
    - accept the first workable one.
- **P   PLAN AND PRACTICE**
  - A better way of behaving.
  - Praise new behavior/better decisions.

Source: Adapted from Miller Liebe, Tissiere, & Bialek 2017

Here, too, it is helpful to check our own mindsets about motivation. We sometimes fall into the habit of thinking about and referring to motivation as if it is a fixed attribute of a child or adolescent (or adult, for that matter).

> You're so lucky, you have Jenn this year. She is such a motivated student. Good luck with Ryan this year. I had him last year and he is so unmotivated.

Inherent in statements like this is the assumption that because Jenn did, and Ryan didn't, actively engage with the classroom material in year one, she is and he isn't likely to do so in year two. And, there may be some truth in this—past behavior does tend to predict future behavior. But this mindset oversimplifies the matter in a way that may not be good for either Jenn or Ryan. Ryan is likely motivated at some point in the day; Jenn may be responding to particular elements in the class in year one that might not be present the next year. What is needed, as with all SECD practice, is intentional consideration of the motivational environment.

In fact, when we discuss motivation in a classroom, the real issue most of the time is not motivation in general but motivation to do what the teacher wants, when the teacher wants it, and how the teacher wants it. The child who disrupts likely has highly built-up motivation to disrupt! In this sense, motivation to learn is an inherent attribute. We can't help learning—the question is what are we learning, when, where, and how.

Our goal, then, is to achieve a productive focus on learning tasks in the school context, despite competing motivation to do otherwise. These competing motivations can stem from a variety of sources, some mainly out-of-school, some from within-the-school experiences (such as failure), some from social media, etc. Achieving productive focus requires explanation/rationale for what one is learning. Building the teacher-student relationship helps provide an intermediate reason for children to engage in learning (first do it for me, then gradually you will learn to do it for yourself). A safe, caring, supportive environment that tolerates mistakes and creative answers also helps students focus productively.

Relationships and Trust

Good news: By taking the various relationship-building, community-enhancing steps described throughout this book (and particularly in Chapter 3), you are already well on your way to meeting these basic needs. As Pintrich (2003, p. 675), summarizing a large body of psycho-educational research, put it:

> The pursuit of social goals such as making friends and being responsible (adhering to classroom rules and norms) are related to academic outcomes including effort and achievement. Accordingly, social goals, which are often assumed to distract from academic pursuits, can be harnessed in the service of academic goals.

"Peer pressure"—a term that is generally associated with anti-social behavior—can apply to positive focus as well. Positive focus can become the responsibility of the group. Imagine a classroom in which norms for engagement with work are co-developed by the teacher and the students; where these norms include processes for handling challenges (*"At times, there will be activities that you find less interesting than others, what can we do to help us stay focused even during those times?"*); and where those norms are regularly reviewed (*How are we doing?*). In such a class, working to maintain positive focus becomes standard operating procedure.

The teacher-student relationship also has bearing on motivation, particularly as it relates to trust. There will be moments that try the motivation of any student (and any teacher, for that matter). Trust in the teacher can lead to a sense that "we'll get through this." Moments of low motivation are problems for students and teachers to address jointly; not burdens placed on the shoulders of students who are reprimanded to "get your act together and pay attention."

Challenge: The Goldilocks Zone of Stress and Achievement

While the relational context of motivation is vital, so is the nature of the learning tasks themselves. There is a longstanding tradition of research about the intersection of stress and motivation. Astronomers, in their quest for extraterrestrial life, have come to use the term *Goldilocks zone* to characterize planets that have the "just right" temperature to support intelligent life. Classrooms (which we very much want to be inhabited by intelligent life) have a Goldilocks zone too, a zone of "just right" stress or pressure. While educators sometimes assume that "stress free" is optimal, that only holds true if one defines any amount of stress as problematic. The high end of the Goldilocks zone—too much stress that leads to intense anxiety or depression—is well known. Motivation can suffer as students disengage from the source of their anxiety or give up because they'll never be "good enough." However, in educational theory and practice, it is possible to go too low on a Goldilocks scale, to have too little stress or pressure. When this happens, work is seen as rote and not challenging. No one is invested in the outcome; how one does doesn't really matter. Here, the risk to motivation is one of boredom and disengagement. We can see the Goldilocks zone as parallel to Vygotsky's Zone of Proximal Development. An effective teacher will scaffold learning opportunities that are challenging enough to be engaging, but not so much as to be anxiety-provoking; they must challenge *and* be seen as achievable.

Challenge is also intimately related to *competence* and *perception of competence*, two key, interrelated elements of self-determination theory. Perceptions of incompetence can lead to an unwillingness to take on challenges. Repeated failure at challenges can lead to perceptions of incompetence; however, for some children, it might only take one emotionally-charged failure to fuel a self-attribution of incompetence. A particular risk is that students come to believe that they are unable to ever develop a competency. While a teacher would want to tailor challenge to the "Goldilocks zone" of any student, such tailoring must occur along with scaffolding the process of developing the competencies needed to meet more difficult challenges and creating challenges that can be met with existing levels of competencies.

Optimism

Positive focus is also related to *optimism*. If I am doubtful that my efforts will bear fruit, I am unlikely to be motivated to make those efforts. Your school librarian can help you find books about optimism for any age group. The great classic, of course, is *The Little Engine That Could*. Books like this are an important way to introduce the word "optimism" and explain to students that it means thinking you can do something or learn something, or expecting that something is going to work out well, be fun, etc. It's an important message to give students that, especially when you are not sure about something, it's good to be optimistic. Even if you are not sure about a test or a project, it's good to think it might work out well. It will help put your best energy into what you are doing.

In addition to using readings, here is another activity to boost optimism (Box 9.7).

Meaningful Work

The perception that work is meaningful can also provide motivation to otherwise rote or boring tasks. While this may come as no surprise, it was validated in experimental conditions by researchers who measured, among other things, the actions of teens who were given the opportunity to choose

---

Box 9.7. The Positive Collection

At the end of each day, take a few minutes and ask students to think about and share one thing that went well for them today at school. They can write it on a slip of paper, enter it into a class Optimism Notebook, write it in their journal, or in some other way "collect" it. For students who can't write, they either can say it, draw it, or be able to choose from cards that describe generic things that might have gone well during a school day. In middle and high school, this can be done at the end of the day, during the last home room, and schedules can be adjusted to allow for the two minutes each day this activity can take. It is well worth the time.

The habit of collecting good things, regardless of whether the day was positive or negative overall, will help build students' sense of optimism.

Note: When students do not contribute to the collection, this is a red flag and the teacher or a school support professional should follow up when this happens with any repetition.

Source: Adapted from Miller Liebe, Tissiere, & Bialek 2017

---

between "completing boring math problems (single-digit subtraction) or consuming captivating but time-wasting media" (Yeager et al., 2014, p. 563) such as viral videos or playing video games. In some cases, the researchers took steps that helped convince the participants that the work, though tedious, could potentially be of some use to them. From a series of studies, the authors conclude that seeing a task as meaningful could increase the time spent on it. They conclude that

> when it is difficult to make a task *interesting* it can be helpful to focus on creating personal *meaning* by promoting a prosocial, self-transcendent *purpose* for learning… All told, it seems that when adolescents had a personally important and self-transcendent 'why' for learning they were able to bear even a tedious and unpleasant 'how."
>
> (Yeager et al., 2014, p. 574, italics in the original)

These authors make a notable distinction between a *self-oriented* purpose and a *self-transcendent* purpose. The former relates to students seeing work as meaningful to themselves (e.g., to become a doctor); the latter has to do with a task enabling them to do good and help others (e.g., to discover a cure for Parkinson's disease). While the two often go together, when their effects are isolated through statistical analysis, self-transcendent purpose has a stronger influence on motivation.

One way to help make work meaningful is to involve students in setting goals and making realistic plans to pursue those goals. Holmes and Hwang (2016), studying the implementation of problem-based mathematics instruction, point out that, "if students autonomously set appropriate goals for themselves, employ effective learning strategies, create a conducive learning environment, and pursue help from peers and teachers, they will facilitate their own learning processes in the short and long term" (Holmes & Hwang, 2016, p. 461).

This can also be done with goals for behavioral and academic improvement, and can set the stage for the reflective processes discussed earlier in this chapter. Making an improvement plan can help in this. The general format is to identify the area in which an improvement plan would be created (noting that no matter how skilled students are, there always are areas in which they can improve). Some of the most common areas are Study Skills, Character, SEL Skills, Personal Health, and Citizenship (of one's classroom, school, community). Then:

Step 1: List 1–3 areas in which improvement is desired.
Step 2: For each area, make a short-term action plan for how to make the desired improvement.
Step 3: Set a period of time to revisit the plan and evaluate it, using these dimensions (circle the best answer):

Very Well   OK but Still More to Go   Not Well

Step 4: Create a new action plan and/or generate new areas for improvement.
Step 5: Repeat this process in ongoing ways.

As an example, the Student Study Skills Improvement Plan worksheet (Box 9.8) can help scaffold goal-setting in that area, one that is relevant across content and can help provide the competencies needed to promote success.

A key consideration is to appoint an Improvement Partner, another student in the class or group who will know the plan and work to help their partner take the desired actions. Often, peers see one another in contexts where adults do not, and often are in a good position to support the improvement effort. Improvement Partners can be reciprocal or you can use a round-robin approach as long as everyone has an Improvement Partner and is a Partner to someone else.

Particularly Productive SECD Pedagogies

The central idea of this book is that the seamless integration of SECD and academic content is both achievable and desirable. The techniques described throughout the previous chapters are compatible with a wide range of content-oriented educational methods. For most educators, the integration of SECD and academic content does not mean scrapping one's current practice and starting from scratch in terms of one's pedagogic approach. (And a note to leaders looking to implement SECD in their setting: The perception that one is trying for wholesale change is likely to sabotage implementation efforts.) Rather, teachers can make relatively minor adaptations to address SECD.

Box 9.8. Student Study Skills Improvement Plan

Date: _____   Student: _____

Study Skills You Plan to Improve:

1. _____

2. _____

3. _____

What Will You Do to Try to Improve:

1. _____
   _____

2. _____
   _____

3. _____
   _____

How Well Did Your Plan Go? (circle the best answer)

Very Well   OK but Still More to Go   Not Well

Take a new planning sheet and list your next set of goals. You can choose all new goals, keep some and add some, or keep all of your current goals and work to improve them.

Your Signature: _____

Your Study Partner's Signature: _____

Group Leader's Signature: _____

Source: Adapted from Elias & Bruene Butler 2005c

There are approaches to education, however, which are particularly good exemplars of the intersection of SECD and academics. In this section, we highlight two pedagogies, service learning and group-oriented instruction, that sit at the intersection of many of the skills discussed in previous chapters.

Service Learning and Social Action

Rachael Kessler, in her groundbreaking book *The Soul of Education*, envisions an approach to service learning that "can take students beyond 'rules' to empathy," that goes "beyond fulfilling mandated 'service learning' requirements to finding meaning and purpose through giving." Meaningful service learning, to Kessler, allows students to "discover the compassion that makes humans want to alleviate the suffering of others" (Kessler, 2000, p. 72).

If empathy hinges on knowing about the lives and experiences of other people, then coming into relationship with an array of other people is crucial. Service learning holds great potential to bring students into direct contact with individuals outside of their usual array of peers.

Berman and McCarthy (2006) provide an example from the Hudson, MA public schools, a district that focused on service learning across grade levels. The picture they paint shows both how service learning can be rooted within the academic curriculum *and* help promote empathy. In one example, they discuss the kindergarten Quilt Project. Students create quilts to be given to babies born in homeless shelters. The students design the squares, create messages and decorations, and take a turn bringing the quilt home to show their parents. They develop a book of messages to accompany the quilts.

> This special project, the fourth service-learning project these kindergartners will experience this year, provides the 5- and 6-year-old students with the opportunity to think about people who are in need and to realize that even young children can provide help and make a difference. (Berman & McCarthy, 2006, p. 51)

Moreover, it is tied to the academic curriculum and "provides them with a rich academic instruction about the letter Q, the geometric shapes sewn into the quilt, the writing of a book for a special audience, and the history and cultural meaning of quilts" (Berman & McCarthy, 2006, p. 51). The Quilt Project connects to literacy education as the class read *The Quiltmaker's Gift* (about helping those in need) and *Home Is Where We Live* (about a child in a homeless shelter). During meeting time, the class makes decisions related to the quilt's design. The quilts are picked up by a new or expectant mother from a shelter. Over their years at the school, students have opportunities to reflect on the service learning projects with which they have been involved.

Research about the impact of service learning on empathy, though scant, is generally supportive (Scott & Graham, 2015). As indicated in the Quilt Project example, service learning needs to be more than a one-off; in fact, intentional design, according to recommendations summarized here, is crucial to success (National Commission on Service Learning, 2002; Scott & Graham, 2015). To promote the maintenance of respectful relationships that embody the I-Thou stance described in Chapter 5, service learning should involve an active, meaningful collaboration with individuals from the community receiving services.

Students should have the opportunity to process their experience—its impact on the community, the problem it addressed and ongoing needs related to it, and their own reactions. It is important to validate all feelings. Students—and staff!—may not have uniformly positive reactions. The work may have been physically tiring, the context unfamiliar and frightening. Perhaps some wonder about the actual impact on the community ("*So, we cleaned the grass on the side of the street. There are a hundred other streets that we didn't clean."*). Particularly when issues of ethnicity, race, and/or socioeconomics are involved, students may experience guilt when comparing their lives with those of the people they've helped. An educator that dismisses, or, worse, shames, a student for reacting in this way is showing a lack of the very empathy she would like to see from the student. In fact, the student may actually be experiencing an element of emotional empathy (Chapter 5)—their negative reactions picking up on the distress of those they met. The SECD teachable moment becomes one of emotional identification and regulation—how are you feeling and how can we stay focused on enacting our virtues through service learning?

Service learning doesn't have to take place outside of the building. In fact, understanding the challenges of those within the school community can develop empathy and improve the lives of all involved. In the Hudson, MA school district, all sixth graders take a drama class in which they "discuss and then create living tableau that use pantomime to generate alternative solutions to prejudice, stereotyping, and conflict and to build a classroom environment in which students can examine their own feelings, ideas, ethical principles, and misconceptions about those who seem different." The dramatic products are presented to students and parents, who have an opportunity to talk to the actors about their work. Similarly, we've worked with several schools in which classes have reacted to drab décor by volunteering to create artwork.

Suggestions to capitalize on the SECD potential of service learning (note that similar suggestions are also relevant to social-action activities):

- Start with feelings. When asking students to think about how they can enhance the lives of those in their schools and beyond, build from their own feelings, and those of others, about the current situation.
  - Getting to hear the feelings of those affected first-hand can be a valuable step in building empathy.
- Practice relationship skills when interacting with others around service or social action projects. Prepare for scenarios that will likely be encountered and role play these. For example:
  - *"When we visit the nursing home, we'll probably meet people who don't hear well. How will we use our BEST communication (Chapter 7) most effectively?"*
  - *"We're going to need to present our ideas to the community board at a formal meeting. How might Keep Calm (Chapter 6) and BEST (Chapter 7) help us make the strongest presentation?"*
- Build social problem-solving skills by involving students in planning service learning projects. The Service Learning-Social Action Planning Worksheet (Box 9.9) can be a useful scaffolding tool. (Note that the MOSAIC curriculum contains other lessons for service learning and social action.)
- Process and reflect throughout the experience. Be open to both positive and negative reactions.

Box 9.9. Service Learning-Social Action Planning Worksheet

Write one sentence that describes the problem (or topic) and the goal of discussing this issue.

Think of different ways to address the problem or issue discussed.

Review the options and vote on the top three.

Review each option and write good (pro) and bad (con) things about each one.

Option 1._____

    PROS: (+)

    CONS: (-)

Option 2._____

    PROS: (+)

    CONS: (-)

Option 3._____

    PROS: (+)

    CONS: (-)

Make your choice and describe the idea:

_____

_____

_____

_____

_____

_____

Bringing Action Plan to Life:

- *What materials will we need?*
- *When and where will we work on this?*
- *Who will we need to help us?*
- *How will we see if it's working?*

Source: Adapted from the MOSAIC Curriculum

Group-Oriented Instruction

It should come as no surprise that group-oriented instructional models provide excellent opportunities for promoting SECD. First, a quick guide to the terrain. Classrooms themselves are groups, a type of group we'd like to think of as a community. However, the expectation is that within this group setting assignments are generally completed individually. (Of course, even when students are working individually, there still exists an element of interdependence in the group; the actions of the teacher and of peers can still have an impact on any individual.) At times, teachers will ask students to work with one or more other students to complete a task. Sometimes this happens in an ad hoc manner (*"Now turn to your neighbor and discuss why you think the character made the choice she did"*). Sometimes this is done more formally. Groups may be set ahead of time and may be asked to stay constituted over the course of time (e.g., to work each day for 45 minutes on a project that will be presented at the end of the month). Some approaches to education, such as project-based learning and cooperative learning, are specifically designed to capitalize on the contributions of group members; they are inherently group oriented.

Group learning adds social and emotional complexity to the existing dynamics of a classroom. As such, group-oriented pedagogies provide opportunities for both powerful SECD and academic learning. There are several steps that educators can take to bring the social and emotional elements of the group experience to the forefront, along with the academic goals for the group.

As with SECD promotion in general, proactive preparation for social interaction is fundamental. Johnson and Johnson (1999), whose work plays a central role in discussions of cooperative learning, point out that in order for collaborative groups to succeed, "[p]ersons must be taught the leadership, decision-making, trust-building, communication, and conflict-management skills just as purposefully and precisely as academic skills" (Johnson & Johnson, 1999, p. 71).

It is obvious that students should enter a group-work situation knowing what is expected of them in terms of the product (*"Each group should create a commercial for a new tech product they develop"*). Expectations for the *process* should be clear as well. It is often helpful for students to have specific roles (either assigned by the teacher or chosen by the student). This is particularly the case when there are group members who may be at risk for not being heard. In a study of group work in a math class, for example, Holmes and Hwang (2016, p. 461) found that having assigned roles provided students with "permission to speak within protected guidelines" and "made them feel accepted and comfortable in their designated roles, which may have encouraged more dialogue among diverse group members."

Group learning situations can become opportunities to build SECD skills by having students set SECD-related ground rules before they begin. This can work even if students have already been working in groups. "When difficulties in relating to each other arise, students must engage in group processing and identify, define, and solve the problems they are having working together effectively" (Johnson & Johnson, 1999, p. 71).

Here are questions you can use with students to help them create their own guidelines. These Preparing for Group Work questions can be part of a discussion or can be used as a written group agreement.

- How will we deal with conflict in our group?
- How will be sure that each person's ideas are heard and respected?
- How will we make sure that everyone contributes and what will we do if they don't?

Embarking on group work can also provide opportunities for self-reflection and self-awareness. Educator Larissa Pahomov (2018), for example, recommends what she refers to as an *opening confessional* around a question such as: "What weak spots do you bring to this group, and how can your group mates help you?" and a closing reflection such as "What was your group's greatest strength in this process? Where did your group struggle or fall short? If you could start this process over, what would you do differently, as both an individual and as a group?" If you used the Preparing for Group Work questions, above, use those as the basis for check-ins about the social and emotional elements of a group's work at points throughout the process and when it is complete.

A Final Integrative Example

To close this chapter, we provide one additional example of how several SECD competencies come together to support a more complex behavior. In this case, we focus on a topic that is relevant to classroom functioning in general, Joining a Group.

Joining a New Group

Adapted from SDM/SPS materials (Bruene Butler, Romasz-McDonald, & Elias, 2011; Elias & Bruene Butler, 2005c, 2005b, 2005a).

Objectives

- To teach students guidelines for joining a group.
- To increase awareness of the problems that may be encountered when joining a group.
- To discuss responsibilities of group members when accepting new members.

Materials

- Whole class display of "Joining a New Group" (Box 9.10).

Instructional Activities

1. Introduce the issue: Begin by telling students that you are going to tell them a story about a student who is just about their age and grade. Say something along these lines:

   "Jim has just moved to a new town, so he has to go to a new school. He does not know anyone. During recess, everyone went out to play kickball. Jim wants to play but does not know how to join the group. Let's help him learn to join the group."

   Ask if anyone has ever had to join a group of people that they have never met before. How did it feel?

2. Develop the idea of using a planned set of steps to get into a new group. Explain:

   "Jim can learn some steps to help him join the group. The first thing Jim should do is observe the feelings and actions of the children. Why should he do that?" [Some reasons may be to learn the interests of the children, understand the roles of the fame to get to know the children and so on.]

   "Where would be the best place for Jim to watch from?" (Close by— so the children in the group can see his interest.) *"Now he should find a way to join in. How could he join in?"* (Start a conversation by commenting on what is going on, introduce himself, or look for a way to help or contribute.)

   Have children role play each of the ways Jim could join. Refer to Keep Calm (Chapter 6) and BEST (Chapter 7) to provide feedback when students are conducting a role play to model what they would do to enter a group.

3. Discuss possible problems.

   a. Say: *Sometimes children want to join a group so badly that they may do the wrong things. Sometimes a child may want to observe a group with intentions to join, but may be too shy and stand and stare too long.*

   b. Model a timid body posture and hovering stance and ask:

      i. *"Why isn't this a good idea?* (It makes the others uncomfortable.) *This is an example of a passive behavior."*

   c. Brainstorm other ways that would be wrong when joining a group. Some examples: calling attention to oneself in a disruptive way, interrupting at the wrong time, disagreeing with or negatively criticizing the children.

      i. *These are examples of aggressive behavior.*

4. Point out that nothing is guaranteed to work at once or all the time.
   - *"Sometimes even when you do the right things, the children may ignore you at first. Why may they do that?"* (They may be involved in what they are doing. They may feel shy about newcomers, too.) *"What should you do?"* (Don't take it personally; try again.)
5. Summarize the steps and the responsibility of the group members.
   a. Say: *"Now let's look at Jim's situation again. If you were part of the group, what could you do to make it easier for Jim?"* (Introduce yourself, start a conversation, introduce him to others, ask him to join.)
   b. Make connections between the behaviors that help someone enter a new group successfully and BEST (Chapter 7).
   c. Show the "Joining a New Group" display and review the steps (Box 9.10).
6. Role play some situations where children are asking to join a group.
   a. Here are some possibilities:
      i. Cindy and Brian are playing a game. Alex wants to join. How could Alex ask? What could Cindy and Brian do?
      ii. Terrell is entering middle school. Walking up to the school on the first day he sees only students that he does not know. What can Terrell do while waiting outside for the doors to open?
      iii. Lisette invites Amy to a birthday party. Lisette is the only person Amy knows. How could Amy meet more people? What could Lisette do?
      iv. Willie is new at school. The teacher asks him to find a place to sit at lunchtime. How should Willie join a lunch table? What should children at the table do?
      v. Jackie was in a special classroom and is being mainstreamed to a regular science class. The day she begins the class they are working on a project in groups of four. How can Jackie join the three other students in the group?
7. Introduce a reflective summary.
   a. Ask students to reflect on the question "What did you learn from today's lesson?" Reinforce key themes and review in the future.
8. Plan to promote transfer and generalization of skill.
   a. A review of this activity is useful as part of preparation for transition to a new grade or school, but it can also be used at any time—especially if there are cliques in your class or new students entering.

Tips for Teachers

1. "Joining a New Group" is a difficult skill. Sometimes even the most socially skilled child may experience difficulty or rejection when attempting the techniques it recommends. Research on children's successful entry behavior has consistently found that when children take

time to observe a new group before making any bids to enter, they are most likely to be successful. This observation allows the new child an opportunity to learn about the group and develop a frame of reference for doing what the group is doing. In contrast, prematurely trying to redirect the group is a high-risk activity.

Persistence is also important, as entry is a difficult task for all children, but group acceptance is more likely over time. The skill components targeted in this topic are based on social skills that will help increase children's success, but it is also important to prepare them for the fact that success may take time. Because of this, it can be helpful to have children anticipate obstacles and ways that their attempts to enter a group might not be successful. Brainstorming and role playing ways to handle those situations will help them cope with a range of possible outcomes.

For further reinforcement, have students write a short story about, or discuss situations concerning, joining a group that they have experienced (for example, new neighborhoods, classes, sports teams, scouting, and after-school activities). Ask how they feel if they experienced any problems, and what their goals were. Ask them to remember what they did and what the outcome was. What was successful and what did not work? What would they do differently the next time?

2. Be sure to link the topic of Joining a New Group to virtues (Chapter 2) and/or the discussions of behavioral expectations for your class (Chapter 3).

Box 9.10. Joining a New Group

1. Focus on the ongoing activity.
2. Keep Calm and observe.
3. Look for a way to help or contribute.
4. Be your BEST and introduce yourself.
5. Ask if you can join.

Chapter 10

The Road to Success on the Journey Ahead

Using Feedback and Outreach to Cultivate Support and Build Expertise

Promoting our students' SECD involves setting the conditions most likely to create and sustain the set of dispositions, skills, and competencies that are required for positive development. Through our relationships, the climate we set in our classrooms, and the opportunities for practice and reflection that we provide, we set in motion a growth process. As you've no doubt discovered even before reading this book, there is no quick means of generating SECD growth. Persistence is needed when learning and practicing something new.

The same is true when it comes to educators, for whom the "something new" is the implementation of SECD-enhancing activities in a more structured way in their classrooms. However, the importance of repeated practice, incremental growth, and planning for long-term sustained growth is often overlooked when it comes to teachers themselves. A multi-year scope and sequence of growth is par for the course for student learning. For teacher learning and professional development? Not so much.

Perhaps you've experienced one of the following:

- A one-shot professional development session that leaves you saying, "Sounds like an interesting idea … but now what!?"
- The delivery of a brand-new shrink-wrapped textbook or curriculum guide that makes you wonder what you are supposed to do with everything you've been teaching up to this point.
- A mandate of expectations for implementing some new initiative that has you scratching your head about how you are going to follow through.

These scenarios are unfortunately common, and they have predicable consequences. When you've encountered these situations, how would you describe your reaction:

- Excited about the opportunity to try something new.
- Hopeful that the new initiative will enhance teaching and learning.
- Confused as to what you are actually supposed to do.

- Self-doubt about your ability to fulfill new expectations.
- Skeptical about whether you'll really be held to these new expectations or whether they are just a passing fad.

In all likelihood, your reaction contains elements of all of these feelings. In our experience, however, revolving-door implementation—being introduced to yet another "extremely important, cutting-edge initiative"—without the proper support, training, and learning time, tends to quash the excitement and hope while fostering confusion, self-doubt, and skepticism.

Any new initiative has a "human side" (Evans, 1996). Most specifically to the current context, there are social and emotional considerations for educators implementing social and emotional learning initiatives!

You've read the ideas in this book. Perhaps you've even tried out a few of them. Great start! And a great start needs a great continuation. Even as you are dipping your toes into the water, you can start thinking about how you will go about swimming laps. In this chapter, we'll discuss some steps to take early on that will help smooth the waters.

Create the Big Picture: Your SECD Vision and Mission Statements

As you start implementing SECD in your classroom, it will become important to keep the big picture in mind. Here are two questions for which your answers are essential:

What is your vision of a classroom infused with SECD?
What is your mission in terms of promoting SECD growth?

Knowing your answer to these questions will provide you with guidance at many decision points you will face, and we will outline a number of these below. But there is another reason. Inevitably, you will articulate your work to a number of different constituencies: peers, supervisors, students, and parents. They, too, will need to understand the big picture before they will appreciate the details. Further, the more your approach is shared by your colleagues, the more powerful the influence will be on students and the more likely it is your work will have a transformational effect on your school.

Try to frame the answers to these questions positively ("Students will solve problems peacefully") rather than negatively ("Students won't fight as much"). Your SECD Vision and Mission Statements can be revisited and revised over time. Communicate them repeatedly—especially to yourself.

Once you have articulated your SECD Vision and Mission, take time to reflect on the following questions (adapted from Novick et al., 2002):

- What holds you back from putting the vision into action?
- What would you put on your list of components of a dynamic, caring community of learners?
- What are the actions you most need to take …
  - … in the next week?
  - … in the next two weeks?
  - … in the next month?
  - … in the next 2–3 months?
  - … in preparation for the end of the school year?
  - … in preparation for the start of the next school year?

Moving Forward: A Problem-Solving Framework

The social problem-solving framework, FIG TESPN, that we introduced in Chapter 8 can be helpful in thinking about your way forward. Table 10.1 (adapted from Novick et al., 2002) shows some questions to consider.

Learn Constantly

It goes without saying, but still deserves to be read, that we are learning all the time. As you carry out your SECD work, you will see what seems to be working better and less so, and which individual students or subgroups of students seem to be learning most effectively and are most engaged—or not. And you will make the appropriate changes and continue to learn as you go.

"Assessment" and "evaluation" have, unfortunately but understandably, taken on negative connotations. But we have found that shifting from this mindset (see Figure 10.1) opens up the possibility of using information and feedback in the spirit of continuous improvement.

To aid in this process, we have used a number of tools designed to provide specific feedback about your students' engagement in and learning from your SECD efforts. They cover two areas:

- Process: How did my SECD-promoting efforts go?
- Progress: How are the SECD competences of students changing over time?

Feedback About the Process

To begin with, it is helpful to maintain a process of reflective self-assessment of SECD efforts. Establishing the habit of reflective practice is core to this endeavor. The following are some general reflection questions to guide your

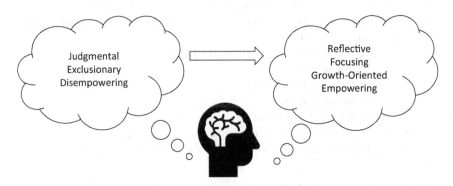

Figure 10.1 Mindset Needed for Assessment and Evaluation

Table 10.1 A Problem-Solving Framework for Action

Step	Description
Readiness: Assess your readiness for change	To what degree do you embrace the SECD theories outlined earlier in this book? How about your supervisors? What might you need to learn more about and how can you do so?
Recognize Feelings: Know when to start problem solving	As you go through your school day in your classroom, when do you experience pride? Frustration? This can provide clues as to areas in need of change.
Identify Problems: Look at the current situation	How might relationships within your classroom contribute to the negative emotions you experience? What are your classroom's strengths and points of pride?
Set Goals: Focus the change efforts	What problems and strengths may be interrelated? What is most important to promoting teaching and learning?
Generate Options: Think of many things to do	What options exist? How can you best create a situation to research this?
Envision Outcomes: Consider all the consequences	For each option, what are the potential outcomes, both positive and negative, that can result? How might outcomes differ for different constituents (e.g., students, parents, etc.)?
Choose Carefully: Select a goal-oriented or goal-driven solution	Given the potential consequences, which option best fits the goals you set?
Plan Prescriptively: Anticipate all details and roadblocks	What are some first steps that you can take in your plan?
Learn Constantly: Obtain feedback and modify accordingly	How will you track the progress and outcomes of your initiative? How will this be integrated into ongoing teaching and learning?

thinking as you implement your SECD activities (adapted from Novick et al., 2002):

☐ What did you like about what you did? What did not go the way you planned?
☐ What happened that you were not expecting?
☐ What would you do differently next time? What will you do next? What else might you do?
☐ How else can you do that/how else can that be done/how have others done this?
☐ What would it take for you to be confident of success?
☐ How did you decide to do what you did?
☐ What do you believe accounts for the outcomes that occurred?

Further, we suggest that these reflections be collected in a way that allows them to be useful for future planning. A structured reflective framework can be useful, as can a portfolio (online or paper) in which to collect reflections. The Curriculum Reflection Sheet (Box 10.1) can be a useful reflective tool.

Box 10.1. Curriculum Reflection Sheet

Teacher/leader:

Date:

Class period and group:

1. General outline of lesson or class activities:
2. Student reactions to this session (for whom was it most or least effective):
3. Most effective or favorable aspects of this session:
4. Least effective or favorable aspects of this session:
5. Points to follow up in next meeting:
6. Points to follow up in the following weeks outside group meetings (that is, in other class periods, other school settings, outside of school):
7. Suggested changes in this activity for the future:

Source: Adapted from material from the Social Decision Making/Social Problem Solving program

---

Your students' reactions to your SECD-enhancing efforts are also important to gauge. Below is a feedback form used in the Social Decision Making/Social Problem Solving program (see Box 10.2). Feel free to adapt it as needed.

Box 10.2. Student Opinion of Social Decision-Making Activities

For Elementary Level

Name: _____ Leader: _____
Date: _____

1. I thought the Social Decision-Making activities were (circle one):
   a. lots of fun
   b. pretty good
   c. OK
   d. no fun at all

2. I would like to have activities like this (circle one):
   a. more often
   b. just like we had them
   c. once in a while
   d. never again

3. What were the best things about the activities?

4. What would make the activities better?

For the following questions, circle YES or NO.

5. The activities have helped me to:
a. get to know students in my class better	YES	NO
b. handle my problems better	YES	NO
c. do better in math	YES	NO
d. feel happier	YES	NO
e. like my teacher more	YES	NO
f. stay calmer	YES	NO
g. better understand things I read	YES	NO

6. I use the things I learned in the Social Decision-Making activities
   when I am:
a. in class	YES	NO
b. at lunch	YES	NO
c. at gym	YES	NO
d. in the hallway (between classes)	YES	NO
e. at home, with my parents	YES	NO
f. at home, with my brothers and sisters	YES	NO
g. with my friends	YES	NO

7. Please write about one or two times you used what you learned in social
   decision-making activities to help you with a problem at school or at
   home. Tell how you solved the problem and what was most helpful to you.
   (Use another sheet of paper if you have to.)

For Upper Grades

Your Grade:

Your Homeroom/Advisory Teacher:

Please answer these questions about social decision making as carefully and honestly as you can.

1. What are some things you remember learning in your social decision-making activities?

Please circle the best answer to the following questions.

2. How often do you use social decision-making skills at school or at home?

   Not at all   Once or twice   Sometimes   Many times   All the time

3. What parts of the lesson/activity did you like most? Least?

4. How useful are the skills you learned in social decision-making activities?

   Not at all   Used them,   Useful   Very useful   Extremely useful
                  but they were
                  not very useful

5. Please describe a time when you used what you learned in social decision making (for example, if you stopped to "Keep Calm" when you were nervous or upset, or used FIG TESPN to think about how to handle a problem). Use the back of this paper if you need to.

6. What goals have you set for yourself for using social decision-making skills through the rest of the year and/or summer?

Source: Adapted by Sue Coen, Ron Durkin, and Linda Bruene Butler, Berkley Heights New Jersey from SDM/SPS materials (Bruene Butler, Romasz-McDonald, & Elias 2011; Elias & Bruene Butler, 2005c, 2005b, 2005a)

Feedback About Progress

Tracking student progress can provide vital information to inform where to best focus your efforts. What follows is a variety of tools that you can adapt for your own use. Keep in mind that these examples came from initiatives aimed at developing the skills listed in these assessments. Your assessments should reflect the goals of *your* efforts. Be sure to note patterns that might reflect differential learning in student subgroups, as well as persistent patterns of problems in a particular student that might necessitate Tier 2 intervention. Our examples include:

- The Profile of Social Decision Making Strengths (Box 10.3), a class-level form that can be used as a pre/post assessment.
- The Adult Assessment of Student SDM/SPS Skills (Box 10.4), and individual level form that can also be used as a pre/post assessment.
- The EQ Quiz for Students (Box 10.5), which can be used for students from grade 4 and older.

Box 10.3. Profile of Social Decision-Making Strengths (Pre-/Post-Test)

Teacher: _____   Date: _____

School: _____   Grade Level: _____

Record your observation for the students in your class as a group indicating the percentage of students in your class that demonstrate mastery of the following skills.

Please **circle** percentage for the following:

Listen carefully:	10% 20% 30% 40% 50% 60% 70% 80% 90% 100%
Accurately remember what others say:	10% 20% 30% 40% 50% 60% 70% 80% 90% 100%
Follow directions:	10% 20% 30% 40% 50% 60% 70% 80% 90% 100%
Concentrate and follow through on tasks:	10% 20% 30% 40% 50% 60% 70% 80% 90% 100%
Calm him or herself down:	10% 20% 30% 40% 50% 60% 70% 80% 90% 100%
Carry on a conversation without upsetting or provoking others:	10% 20% 30% 40% 50% 60% 70% 80% 90% 100%
Accept praise or approval:	10% 20% 30% 40% 50% 60% 70% 80% 90% 100%
Choose praiseworthy and caring friends:	10% 20% 30% 40% 50% 60% 70% 80% 90% 100%
Know when help is needed:	10% 20% 30% 40% 50% 60% 70% 80% 90% 100%
Ask for help when needed:	10% 20% 30% 40% 50% 60% 70% 80% 90% 100%
Work as part of a problem-solving team:	10% 20% 30% 40% 50% 60% 70% 80% 90% 100%
Recognize signs of feelings in self:	10% 20% 30% 40% 50% 60% 70% 80% 90% 100%
Recognize signs of feelings in others:	10% 20% 30% 40% 50% 60% 70% 80% 90% 100%
Accurately describe a range of feelings:	10% 20% 30% 40% 50% 60% 70% 80% 90% 100%

Clearly put problems into words:	10%	20%	30%	40%	50%	60%	70%	80%	90%	100%
State realistic interpersonal goals:	10%	20%	30%	40%	50%	60%	70%	80%	90%	100%
Think of several ways to solve a problem or reach a goal:	10%	20%	30%	40%	50%	60%	70%	80%	90%	100%
Think of different types of solutions:	10%	20%	30%	40%	50%	60%	70%	80%	90%	100%
Differentiate short- and long-term consequences:	10%	20%	30%	40%	50%	60%	70%	80%	90%	100%
Determine the effects of actions on self and others:	10%	20%	30%	40%	50%	60%	70%	80%	90%	100%
Keep positive and negative possibilities in mind:	10%	20%	30%	40%	50%	60%	70%	80%	90%	100%
Select solutions that can reach goals:	10%	20%	30%	40%	50%	60%	70%	80%	90%	100%
Make choices that do not harm self or others:	10%	20%	30%	40%	50%	60%	70%	80%	90%	100%
Consider details before carrying out a solution (who, when, where, with whom, etc.):	10%	20%	30%	40%	50%	60%	70%	80%	90%	100%
Anticipate obstacles:	10%	20%	30%	40%	50%	60%	70%	80%	90%	100%
Respond appropriately when plans are thwarted:	10%	20%	30%	40%	50%	60%	70%	80%	90%	100%
Try out his or her ideas:	10%	20%	30%	40%	50%	60%	70%	80%	90%	100%
Learn from experience or from seeking out input from adults and friends:	10%	20%	30%	40%	50%	60%	70%	80%	90%	100%
Use previous experience to help "next time":	10%	20%	30%	40%	50%	60%	70%	80%	90%	100%

Comments:

Source: Adapted by Sue Coen, Ron Durkin, and Linda Bruene Butler, Berkley Heights New Jersey from SDM/SPS materials (Bruene Butler, Romasz-McDonald, & Elias 2011; Elias & Bruene Butler 2005c, 2005b, 2005a)

Box 10.4. Adult Assessment of Student SDM/SPS Skills

A. Readiness Area	To What Extent Can This Child	Observation
		(circle one)
1. Self-control	a. Listen carefully and accurately	1　2　3
	b. Remember and follow directions	1　2　3
	c. Concentrate and follow through on tasks	1　2　3
	d. Calm himself or herself down	1　2　3
	e. Carry on a conversation without upsetting or provoking others	1　2　3
2. Social Awareness	a. Accept praise or approval	1　2　3
	b. Choose praiseworthy and caring friends	1　2　3
	c. Know when help is needed	1　2　3
	d. Ask for help when needed	1　2　3
	e. Work as part of a problem-solving team	1　2　3
B. Social Decision-Making Area		
1. Feelings	a. Recognize signs in self	1　2　3
	b. Recognize signs in others	1　2　3
	c. Accurately describe a range of feelings	1　2　3
2. Problem	a. Clearly put problems into words	1　2　3
3. Goal	a. State realistic interpersonal goals	1　2　3
4. Alternatives	a. Think of several ways to solve a problem or reach a goal	1　2　3
	b. Think of different types of solutions	1　2　3
	c. Do (a) and (b) for different types of problems	1　2　3
5. Consequences	a. Differentiate short- *and* long-term consequences	1　2　3
	b. Look at effects on self *and* others	1　2　3

	c. Keep positive *and* negative possibilities in mind	1	2	3
6. Choose	a. Select solutions that can reach goals	1	2	3
	b. Make choices that do not harm self or others	1	2	3
7. Plan and Check	a. Consider details before carrying out a solution (who, when, where, with whom, etc.)	1	2	3
	b. Anticipate obstacles	1	2	3
	c. Respond appropriately when plans are thwarted	1	2	3
8. Learn for Next Time	a. Try out his or her ideas	1	2	3
	b. Learn from experience or from seeking out input from adults and friends	1	2	3
	c. Use previous experience to help "next time"	1	2	3

Box 10.5. EQ Quiz for Students

Name:

Date:

EQ is a short way of referring to emotional intelligence. Your IQ helps you learn school subjects and other information, and your EQ helps you deal with feelings, relationships, problems, choices, and goals. EQ is something you can learn and get better at, and it is even more important to your happiness and success than your IQ is. This "quiz" will help you get an idea of where you are right now in terms of your EQ. As you fill out this form, try not to compare yourself to others or say what you think other people want to hear. Instead, base your answers on what you really think about yourself, and try to be as honest with yourself as you can. You will not be graded on this. The information can help you understand yourself better and will help you identify skills you would like to work on more.

    For each statement, give yourself:

  3 points if the statement is definitely true

  2 points if the statement is sometimes true or sort of true

  1 point if the statement is rarely true or not true

1. I am comfortable with talking about my emotions.   3☐ 2☐ 1☐
2. I know lots of words to describe my feelings.   3☐ 2☐ 1☐
3. I can tell how other people are feeling.   3☐ 2☐ 1☐
4. I care about how other people are feeling.   3☐ 2☐ 1☐
5. I usually have a positive attitude about myself, even when I face challenges.   3☐ 2☐ 1☐
6. I can manage my emotions and reactions in difficult situations.   3☐ 2☐ 1☐
7. I can wait patiently for something I really want.   3☐ 2☐ 1☐
8. I have reasonable goals.   3☐ 2☐ 1☐
9. I have clear ideas about how I can reach those goals.   3☐ 2☐ 1☐
10. I can communicate my ideas assertively and respectfully.   3☐ 2☐ 1☐
11. I listen attentively when other people are speaking.   3☐ 2☐ 1☐
12. I know what I need and how to ask for it.   3☐ 2☐ 1☐
13. I know how to solve problems independently.   3☐ 2☐ 1☐
14. I am comfortable being in a group of kids my own age.   3☐ 2☐ 1☐

- Take a look at your 3s. These are some of your strengths. Congratulations! Be aware of these skills, especially in challenging situations, and keep working on them.

- Next, take a look at your 2s. You have some ability in these skills, but you could use more practice. You can build on what you already know to get better at these skills with time.

- Now take a look at your 1s. These skills will take you more time to develop and strengthen. We all have skills that are harder for us than others. To get better at these, you can focus on them and work on them, both by yourself and with the support of others.

Source: Adapted from Elias and Tobias 2018

Maintain a Problem-Solving Mindset

You've assessed and, inevitably, you've identified—along with successes—some areas that could use some improvement. Your students' path to SECD growth will not be linear—there will be moments in which an educator will feel great satisfaction at their progress and times of great frustration at the lack thereof. This will be the case for even the most seasoned SECD veteran.

Importantly, *your* path to promoting SECD growth among your students will not be linear—there will be moments in which you feel great satisfaction in your work and times of great frustration when things don't go as planned. Again, this is the case for even the more seasoned SECD veteran. While you can't know for sure what the roadblocks will be, it is worth thinking about what might happen and how you can handle challenges that arise (Box 10.6).

Box 10.6. Roadblocks to Sustainability

W. G. Tierney (2001) and the National Center for Education and Innovation (1999) have found that resistance can often be traced to a set of organizational factors.

1. People do not agree on the problem to be solved/goal to be pursued.
2. Time frames and working structures are not clear.
3. There is little accountability, monitoring, benchmarks for implementation.
4. Changes are not communicated or if they are, it is not done with perspective and care.
5. The system is frozen—people come to feel "why bother" and nothing happens/changes.
6. Resistant attitudes, misconceptions, and priorities.
7. Logistical barriers: funding, training, etc.

Source: Adapted from Novick, Kress, & Elias 2002

Of the above, circle the roadblock (or roadblocks) that you anticipate posing the most difficulty in your setting.

Tierney (2001), Elias and Berkowitz (2016), and Novick, Kress, & Elias (2002) have suggested remedies for "unsticking" each of the most common organizational roadblocks.

1. **Foster an atmosphere of agreement.** Reopen discussions to a limited degree, but more broadly if necessary. Reconsider goals. Be sure excluded voices have a say, especially opinion leaders, but mobilize positive opinion leaders to visibly engage in the discussions to illustrate the consensus already achieved.
2. **Define roles and time frames.** Specify who is going to do what, by when. Find out who cannot carry out all of their role(s) and make plans around it. Create a spirit in which creating a chance is more important than not disclosing that one cannot do what is expected.
3. **Seek comparative data.** Look at how similar institutions do similar things. Seek out advice from mentors. However, give credit for your own progress.

4. **Ensure good communication.** Discuss how information will be disseminated, how and by whom. Frequent communication is essential early in the implementation process, and set up acknowledgements that communications have been received.

5. **Encourage an innovation-friendly culture.** Help people see change in a positive context, in the spirit of continuous improvement. Adaptation to changing realities is an ethical and professional responsibility. So is providing them with safe, caring, challenging, and supportive learning environments to which all students can feel connected and contributing. Of course, the same is true for staff.

6. **Address myths directly.** Resistant attitudes most often come from misunderstandings. Foremost is that this is the responsibility of parents, not educators. As we now know, educators require social-emotionally competent students with good character if they are to achieve academic success and more for their students. Relying on parents to provide this essential educational element is a recipe for continued struggle, if not outright failure. Often, this myth hides a deeper uncertainty about teaching SECD. This is understandable, and ultimately can be overcome by showing educators what SECD looks like in other schools, all the states and schools that are pursuing SECD and experiencing academic success, and creating structures of support as people develop this new area of expertise (which actually requires very little that is different from the skills needed to be an effective educator).

7. **Create a strong school identity and then plan to live it.** Money, time, and other resources can always be found for priorities. Starting out with a compelling vision for how one's school can be often galvanizes efforts to make that happen. A wider vision tends to gather more support than a focus on smaller, individual programs that show no promise toward making lasting changes in the school and how staff, students, parents, and the wider community perceive it. We discuss this later when we talk about creating Schools of Character (also elaborated by Elias & Berkowitz, 2016).

Novick, Kress, and Elias (2002) also recommend a problem-solving process as a guide to overcoming these challenges:

1. What is the obstacle to be overcome?
2. What is the long-range goal?
3. What are some possible solutions?
4. What are the advantages and disadvantages of each solution?
5. On balance, what is the best solution?
6. What will I need to do to put that solution into action?
7. What roadblocks do I anticipate and how will I deal with those?

Seek Additional Resources

There are many SECD-enhancing steps that you can take based on the material in this book. Should you want further resources, there are many that are readily available. If your school is interested in coordinating efforts among a number of educators doing SECD work in your setting, it could be helpful to build from an established curriculum or programmatic initiative. Some of these are available as published curriculum guides, some are accompanied by professional development. The website for the Collaborative for Academic, Social, and Emotional Leaning (CASEL.org) has information about programs whose impact have been rigorously evaluated.

In general, look for SECD-related programs that:

- Are grounded in theory and research.
- Teach children to apply SECD skills and ethical values in daily life.
- Build connection to school through caring, engaging classroom and school practices.
- Provide developmentally and culturally appropriate instruction.
- Help schools coordinate and unify programs that are often fragmented.
- Enhance school performance by addressing the affective and social dimensions of academic learning.
- Involve families and communities as partners.
- Establish organizational support and policies that foster success.
- Provide high-quality staff development and support.
- Incorporate continuing evaluation and improvement.

(Based on "Safe and Sound", CASEL, www.casel.org)

You also will find examples at www.character.org. Character.org administers a National Schools of Character program that sets out criteria for what constitutes a "school of character" and a process for application and review. Many states have a State Schools of Character program. This means that you can look for schools in settings like yours and see what they have done to earn their status. (There also is a District of Character program, to recognize when multiple schools in a system are systematically improving students' SECD and culture and climate.) As of this writing, New Jersey and Missouri continue to jockey back and forth to see which state has the most schools of character. In addition, Character.org recognized Promising Practices, representing an effort taking place in some aspect of a school (either at a grade level, or a limited practice that is school-wide or across a particular subject area or part of the school day), to encourage schools to continue on the path to becoming a School of Character. For individual teachers doing SECD, Promising Practices with like-minded colleagues can be an attainable first step and the recognition often piques others' interest toward moving toward another Promising Practice and eventually becoming a School of Character. Indeed, many of the ideas presented in this book can be the foundation of a Promising Practices Award and, combined, can provide a blueprint for a School of Character.

Build and Share Expertise

The classic "egg carton" metaphor continues to hold true: It is often the case that teachers work in close proximity to one another, yet have few opportunities to work *together*. For SECD work—or embarking on any new implementation journey—it is helpful to have partners along the way. At the very least, you'll have the opportunity to share the ups and downs of the process. Even better, your fellow travelers can become a team that helps stimulate creative thinking, problem solves solutions to difficult situations, and shares tips and ideas.

The first step, of course, is to connect with like-minded colleagues in your school. Who else is doing work in the SECD arena? Who else might be interested in undertaking this work, but may need someone (you, that is) to seed the idea and get them involved? As noted, developing your own expertise in a mutual-aid cohort is a powerful step, and applying for a Promising Practices Award (or a similar recognition that often occurs through state and local branches of teachers' associations, such as the National Education Association and the United Federation of Teachers) can provide a tangible focus for your collaboration. Perhaps you can form a Professional Learning Community (PLC) within your school, or even across schools in your district or you can request special summer Professional Development (PD) to build expertise in this area.

A second step is to connect with people outside your school. In addition to searching out Schools of Character in your state, you might also want to check out www.SEL4US.org. SEL4US is a national networking organization with state affiliates in 20 states and increasing, as of this writing. At SEL4US, you can see if there is an SEL4 in your state (e.g., SEL4WA, SEL4MA, SEL4TX, SEL4NJ, SELFL, SEL4OR, SEL4AZ, SEL4IL, SEL4CA) or if there is a beginning effort to build one in your state that you might want to join. The point of SEL4 organizations is to build and share expertise, minimize the reinvention of the wheel, and create a networked improvement community that can accelerate the progress of expert practice through collective collaboration. You also can check the Collaborating States Initiative at the CASEL website to see what progress your state is making in developing standards or guidelines for SEL/SECD policy in your state.

Finally, the Academy for SEL in Schools (SELinSchools.org) maintains two certificate programs for educators; one for SECD Instruction and one for SECD School Leadership. In each case, the online certificate with live chats uses a cohort approach to create collaborative, supportive expertise in a key aspect of SECD. Upon achieving the certificate, educators enter a virtual PLC, where they can get ongoing, real-time consultation with regard to the problems of practice/implementation challenges they inevitably will be experiencing. Of course, the Academy is linked to SEL4US,

CASEL, Character.org, and other SECD-related resources, and therefore, so are participants.

Through these mechanisms, you can take an expansive view of your support team in building and sharing your SECD expertise. Whether or not your school is committed to moving forward, you can be part of a community of practice that will support your work and that will expect you to share insights and practices that you find are working. It is of particular value to connect with those who are at a similar stage in the development of their SECD work, as well as those who are more experienced. This job-embedded PD is ultimately more effective than workshop-based PD.

A Final Reflection: What Characterizes and Unites Those Who Succeed in Building Students' Social-Emotional and Character Competencies?

Our dear colleague and mentor, the late Dr. Bernard Novick, was dedicated to improving the lives of students. He worked with youth in schools in many capacities, and was a leader of Jewish youth groups and respected as such across the United States and in Canada. He was a great observer and trainer of adults who worked with students, and he noticed nine attributes that characterized those who were most successful in their SECD work. We present them in conclusion for you to use in your own reflection, for times when you feel your commitment wavering, or perhaps when your colleagues don't seem to "get it" and you are not sure how to address it. More to the point, you will find allies in your work, to support you and be supported by you, to the extent to which their perspectives match those below. Like Bernie, we believe that these are the attributes every educator should espouse and aspire to if they are to be of optimal guidance to our students, who are our future.

> They feel pride in what they are doing.
> They are taking actions that link with their value systems.
> They believe that their efforts will create a better world for those they care about.
> They possess positive energy, positive sense of well-being.
> They have the skills necessary to carry out SEL/SECD activities.
> They discover they have a lot to contribute.
> They see and hear about their "next door neighbors" doing it.
> They feel a sense of Civic Responsibility.
> They experience deep dissatisfaction with children's problems.
> Source: Novick, Kress, & Elias 2002

To paraphrase one of Bernie's heroes, the sage Hillel:

> If not you as catalyst for SECD for your students, who? If not now, when?

References

Adelman, H. S., & Taylor, L. (2005). Classroom climate. In S. W. Lee (Ed.), *Encyclopedia of School Psychology*. Thousand Oaks, CA: Sage.

Allday, R. A., & Pakurar, K. (2007). Effects of teacher greetings on student on-task behavior. *Journal of Applied Behavior Analysis*, 40(2), 317–320.

Atmatzidou, S., Demetriadis, S., & Nika, P. (2018). How does the degree of guidance support students' metacognitive and problem solving skills in educational robotics? *Journal of Science Education & Technology*, 27(1), 70–85.

Azzam, A. M. (2009). Why creativity now? A conversation with Sir Ken Robinson. *Educational Leadership*, 67(1), 22–26.

Balistreri, K. S., & Alvira-Hammond, M. (2016). Adverse childhood experiences, family functioning and adolescent health and emotional well-being. *Public Health*, 132, 72–78. https://doi.org/10.1016/j.puhe.2015.10.034

Barton, K. C., & Levstik, L. S. (2004). *Teaching History for the Common Good*. Mahwah, NJ: Lawrence Erlbaum Associates.

Bear, G., Mantz, L., & Harris, A. (2019). Peer Relationships: Helping Handout for School. In G. Bear & K. Minke (Eds.), *Helping Handouts: Supporting Students at School and Home* (p. S2H16). Bethesda: MD: NASP.

Belland, B. R., Gu, J., Kim, N. J., & Turner, D. J. (2016). An ethnomethodological perspective on how middle school students addressed a water quality problem. *Educational Technology Research and Development*, 64(6), 1135–1161. https://doi.org/10.1007/s11423-016-9451-8

Berman, S., & McCarthy, M. H. (2006). The connection between character, service, and social-emotional learning. In M. J. Elias & H. A. Arnold (Eds.), *Emotional Intelligence and Academic Achievement* (pp. 46–57). Thousand Oaks, CA: Corwin.

Brady, K., Forton, M. B., Porter, D., & Wood, C. (2003). *Rules in School*. Greenfield, MA: Northeast Foundation for Children.

Bruene Butler, L., Romasz-McDonald, T., & Elias, M. J. (2011). *Social Decision Making/Social Problem Solving: A Curriculum for Academic, Social, and Emotional Learning, Grades K-1*. Champaign, IL: Research Press.

Cantor, P., Osher, D., Berg, J., Steyer, L., & Rose, T. (2018). Malleability, plasticity, and individuality: How children learn and develop in context. *Applied Developmental Science*. https://doi.org/10.1080/10888691.2017.1398649

Comer, J. P. (1980). *School Power: Implications of an Intervention Project*. New York: Free Press.

Dahlsgaard, K., Peterson, C., & Seligman, M. E. P. (2005). Shared virtue: The convergence of human strengths across culture and history. *Review of General Psychology, 9*(3), 203–213.

Dewey, J. (1938). *Experience and Education.* New York: Touchstone.

Drapeau, P. (2014). *Sparking Student Creativity: Practical Ways to Promote Innovative Thinking and Problem Solving.* Alexandria, VA: Association for Supervision and Curriculum Development.

Duckworth, A. L. (2016). *Grit: The Power of Passion and Perseverance.* New York: Scribner.

Eisenberg, N. (2000). Emotion, regulation, and moral development. *Annual Review of Psychology,* 665.

Elias, M. J. (2004). Strategies to infuse social and emotional learning into academics. In J. E. Zins, R. P. Weissberg, M. C. Wang, & H. J. Walberg (Eds.), *Building Academic Success on Social and Emotional Learning* (pp. 113–134). New York: Teachers College Press.

Elias, M. J., & Arnold, H. A. (2006). *The Educator's Guide to Emotional Intelligence and Academic Achievement: Social-Emotional Learning in the Classroom.* Thousand Oaks, CA: Corwin.

Elias, M. J., & Berkowitz, M. W. (2016). *Schools of Social-Emotional Competence and Character: Actions for School Leaders, Teachers, and School Support PRofessionals.* Naples, FL: National Professional Resources.

Elias, M. J., & Bruene Butler, L. (2005a). *Social Decision Making/Social Problem Solving: A Curriculum for Academic, Social, and Emotional Learning, Grades 2–3.* Champaign, IL: Research Press.

Elias, M. J., & Bruene Butler, L. (2005b). *Social Decision Making/Social Problem Solving: A Curriculum for Academic, Social, and Emotional Learning, Grades 4–5.* Champaign, IL: Research Press.

Elias, M. J., & Bruene Butler, L. (2005c). *Social Decision Making/Social Problem Solving for Middle School Students: Skills and Activities for Academic, Social, and Emotional Learning.* Champaign, IL: Research Press.

Elias, M. J., Kranzler, A., Parker, S. J., Kash, V. M., & Weissberg, R. P. (2014). The complementary perspectives of social and emotional learning, moral education, and character education. In L. Nucci, D. Narvaez, & T. Krettenauer (Eds.), *Handbook of Moral and Character Education* (2nd ed., pp. 272–289). Philadelphia, PA: Taylor & Francis.

Elias, M. J., & Tobias, S. E. (2018). *Boost Emotional Intelligence in Students: 30 Flexible Research-Based Activities to Build EQ Skills (Grades 5–9).* Minneapolis, MN: Free Spirit Press.

Elias, M. J., Zins, J. E., & Graczyk, P. A. (2003). Implementation, Sustainability, and Scaling Up of Social-Emotional and Academic Innovations in Public Schools. *School Psychology Review, 32*(3), 303–319.

Elkind, D. (1988). *The Hurried Child: Growing Up Too Fast, Too Soon* (Revised Edition). Reading, MA: Addison-Wesley.

Endacott, J., & Brooks, S. (2013). An updated theoretical and practical model for promoting historical empathy. *Social Studies Research and Practice, 8*(1), 41–58.

Evans, R. (1996). *The Human Side of School Change: Reform, Resistance, and the Real-Life Problems of Innovation.* San Francisco, CA: Jossey-Bass.

Fahy, M., Kupperman, J., & Stanzler, J. (n.d.). *Simulation and the Complex Geography of Learning.* Unpublished manuscript.

Foley, A. E., Herts, J. B., Borgonovi, F., Guerriero, S., Levine, S. C., & Beilock, S. L. (2017). The math anxiety-performance link: A global phenomenon. *Current Directions in Psychological Science*, 26(1), 52–58. https://doi.org/10.1177/0963721416672463

Goleman, D. (1995). *Emotional Intelligence*. New York: Bantam.

Graesser, A. C., Fiore, S. M., Greiff, S., Andrews-Todd, J., Foltz, P. W., & Hesse, F. W. (2018). Advancing the science of collaborative problem solving. *Psychological Science in the Public Interest*, 19(2), 59–92. https://doi.org/10.1177/1529100618808244

Gross, J. J. (2015). Emotion regulation: Current status and future prospects. *Psychological Inquiry*, 26(1), 1–26. https://doi.org/10.1080/1047840X. 2014.940781

Hoerr, T. R. (2018). Building empathy in schools: In an era of rancor and polarization, let's foster empathy in our schools. *Educational Leadership*, 75(7), 86–87.

Holmes, V.-L., & Hwang, Y. (2016). Exploring the effects of project-based learning in secondary mathematics education. *Journal of Educational Research*, 109(5), 449–463.

Jackson, P. W., Boorstrom, R. E., & Hansen, D. T. (1993). *The Moral Life of Schools*. San Francisco, CA: Jossey-Bass.

Jacobson, L. (2017). Teach students resilience, empathy, and more with social emotional learning strategies. *School Library Journal*. Retrieved from www.slj.com/?detailStory=teach-students-resilience-empathy-and-more-with-social-emotional-learning-strategies

Jennings, P. A. (2015). *Mindfulness for Teachers: Simple Skills for Peace and Productivity in the Classroom*. New York: Norton & Co.

Jennings, P. A., & Greenberg, M. T. (2009). The prosocial classroom: Teacher social and emotional competence in relation to student and classroom outcomes. *Review of Educational Research*, 79(1), 491–525. https://doi.org/10.3102/0034654308325693

Johnson, D. W., & Johnson, R. T. (1999). Making cooperative learning work. *Theory Into Practice*, 38(2), 67–73.

Katz, M., & Kress, J. S. (2018). Jewish history engagement in an on-line simulation: Golda and Coco, Leah and Lou at the Jewish Court of All Time. *Journal of Jewish Education*, 84(2), 196–221.

Kelly, J. G. (1979). Tain't what you do, it's the way that you do it. *American Journal of Community Psychology*, 7, 239–261.

Kessler, R. (2000). *The Soul of Education: Helping Students Find Connection, Compassion, and Character at School*. Alexandria, VA: Association for Supervision and Curriculum Development.

Kolovelonis, A., Goudas, M., & Dermitzaki, I. (2011). The effect of different goals and self-recording on self-regulation of learning a motor skill in a physical education setting. *Learning and Instruction*, 21(3), 355–364. https://doi.org/10.1016/j.learninstruc.2010.04.001

Lamy, C. (2013). *American Children in Chronic Poverty: Complex Risks, Benefit-Cost Analyses, and Untangling the Knot*. Lanham, MD: Lexington Books.

Levinson, R. (2018). Introducing socio-scientific inquiry-based learning (SSIBL). *School Science Review*, 100(371), 31–35.

Liljedahl, P. (2016). Building thinking classrooms: Conditions for problem solving. In P. Felmer, E. Pehkonen, & J. Kilpatrick (Eds.), *Posing and Solving Mathematical Problems* (pp. 361–386). Switzerland: Springer.

Long, D. (2019). School leaders' role in empowering teachers through SEL. *State Innovations*, *24*(1), 1–4.

Lutz, A., Slagter, H. A., Dunne, J. D., & Davidson, R. J. (2008). Attention regulation and monitoring in meditation. *Trends in Cognitive Sciences*, *12*(4), 163–169. https://doi.org/10.1016/j.tics.2008.01.005

Mabry, M., & Bhavnagri, N. P. (2012). Perspective taking of immigrant children: Utilizing children's literature and related activities. *Multicultural Education*, *19*(3), 48–54.

Marsh, J. (2012, March 29). Do mirror neurons give us empathy? Retrieved March 22, 2019, from The Greater Good website: https://greatergood.berkeley.edu/article/item/do_mirror_neurons_give_empathy# (accessed 16 October, 2019).

Merritt, E. G., Wanless, S. B., Rimm-Kaufman, S. E., Cameron, C., & Peugh, J. L. (2012). The contribution of teachers' emotional support to children's social behaviors and self-regulatory skills in first grade. *School Psychology Review*, *41*(2), 141–159.

Miller Liebe, C., Tissiere, M., & with Bialek, S. (2017). *Embedding Social and Emotional Learning in High School Classrooms*. Cambridge, MA: Engaging Schools.

Monobe, G., & Son, E. H. (2014). Using Children's Literature and Drama to Explore Children's Lives in the Context of Global Conflicts. *Social Studies*, *105*(2), 69–74. https://doi.org/10.1080/00377996.2013.820164

Mugno, D., & Rosenblitt, D. (2001). Helping emotionally vulnerable children: Moving toward an empathic orientation in the classroom. In J. Cohen (Ed.), *Caring Classrooms/Intelligent Schools: The Social Emotional Education of Young Children* (pp. 59–76). New York: Teachers College Press.

Naftel, M., & Elias, M. J. (1995). Building problem solving and decision making skills through literature analysis. *Middle School Journal*, *26*(4), 7–11.

National Center for Innovation and Education. (1999). *Lessons for Life: How Smart Schools Boost Academic, Social, and Emotional Intelligence*. Bloomington, IN: HOPE Foundation.

National Commission on Service Learning. (2002). *Learning in Deed: The Power of Service-Learning for American Schools*. Retrieved from http://files.eric.ed.gov/fulltext/ED465829.pdf

Nigg, J. T. (2017). On the relations among self-regulation, self-control, executive functioning, effortful control, cognitive control, impulsivity, risk-taking, and inhibition for developmental psychopathology. *Journal of Child Psychology and Psychiatry*, *58*(4), 361–383.

Novick, B., Kress, J. S., & Elias, M. J. (2002). *Building Learning Communities with Character: How to Integrate Academic, Social, and Emotional Learning*. Alexandria, VA: Association for Supervision and Curriculum Development.

Osher, D., Kendziora, K., Spier, E., & Garibaldi, M. L. (2014). School Influences on Child and Youth Development. In Z. Sloboda & H. Petras (Eds.), *Defining Prevention Science* (pp. 151–169). https://doi.org/10.1007/978-1-4899-7424-2_7

Pahomov, L. (2018). Inventories, confessionals, and contracts: Strategies for effective group work. *Educational Leadership*, *76*(1), 34–38.

Pintrich, P. R. (2003). A motivational science perspective on the role of student motivation in learning and teaching contexts. *Journal of Educational Psychology*, *95*(4), 667–686.

Raver, C. C., Blair, C., & Garrett-Peters, P. (2015). Poverty, household chaos, and interparental aggression predict children's ability to recognize and modulate negative emotions. *Development and Psychopathology, 27*(03), 695–708. https://doi.org/10.1017/S0954579414000935

Rozek, C. S., Ramirez, G., Fine, R. D., & Beilock, S. L. (2019). Reducing socio-economic disparities in the STEM pipeline through student emotion regulation. *Proceedings of the National Academy of Sciences, 116*(5), 1553. https://doi.org/10.1073/pnas.1808589116

Saarni, C. (2007). The development of emotional competence: Pathways for helping children to become emotionally intelligent. In R. Bar-On, J. G. Maree, & M. J. Elias (Eds.), *Educating People to Be Emotionally Intelligent* (pp. 15–36). Westport, CT: Praeger.

Sadler, T. D., & Zeidler, D. L. (2004). The significance of content knowledge for informal reasoning regarding socioscientific issues: Applying genetics knowledge to genetic engineering issues. *Science Education, 89*(1), 71–93.

Schmid, P. F. (2001). Comprehension: The art of not knowing. Dialogical and ethical perspectives on empathy as dialogue in personal and person-centred relationships. In S. Haugh & T. Merry (Eds.), *Empathy* (pp. 53–71). Llangarron, UK: PCCS Books.

Scott, K. E., & Graham, J. A. (2015). Service-Learning: Implications for Empathy and Community Engagement in Elementary School Children. *Journal of Experiential Education, 38*(4), 354–372. https://doi.org/10.1177/1053825915592889

Selman, R. L. (2003). *The Promotion of Social Awareness*. New York: Russell Sage Foundation.

Selman, R. L., & Dray, A. (2006). Risk and prevention. In M. H. Bornstein, T. Leventhal, & R. M. Lerner (Eds.), *Handbook of Child Psychology. Vol. 5. Child Psychology in Practice* (5th ed., pp. 378–419). New York: John Wiley & Sons.

Shady, S. L. H., & Larson, M. (2010). Tolerance, empathy, or inclusion? Insights from Martin Buber. *Educational Theory, 60*(1), 81–96.

Sigel, I. E. (1993). The centrality of a distancing model for the development of representational competence. In R. R. Cocking & K. A. Renninger (Eds.), *The Development of Meaning and Psychological Distance* (pp. 141–158). Hillside, NJ: Lawrence Erlbaum.

Sigel, I. E., & Kelly, T. D. (1988). A cognitive developmental approach to questioning. In J. T. Dillon (Ed.), *Questions and Discussion: A Multidisciplinary Study* (pp. 105–134). Norwood, NJ: Ablex.

Sizer, N. F., & Sizer, T. (1999). *The Students Are Watching: Schools and the Moral Contract*. Boston, MA: Beacon Press.

Social and Emotional Learning: A short history. (2011, October 6). Retrieved November 23, 2017, from Edutopia website: www.edutopia.org/social-emotional-learning-history

Stern, R., Hyman, L., & Martin, C. E. (2006). The importance of self-awareness for school counselors. In J. Pellitteri, R. Stern, C. Shelton, & B. Muller-Ackerman (Eds.), *Emotionally Intelligent School Counseling* (pp. 49–62). Mahwah, NJ: Lawrence Erlbaum Associates.

Sutton, R. E., Mudrey-Camino, R., & Knight, C. C. (2009). Teachers' Emotion Regulation and Classroom Management. *Theory Into Practice, 48*(2), 130–137. Retrieved from JSTOR.

Tierney, W. G. (2001). Why committees don't work: Creating a structure for change. *Academe, 87*(3), 25–29.

Vande Zande, R., Warnock, L., Nikoomanesh, B., & Van Dexter, K. (2014). The design process in the art classroom: Building problem-solving skills for life and careers. *Art Education*, *67*(6), 20–27.

White, A. G., & Bailey, J. S. (1990). Reducing disruptive behaviors of elementary physical education students with sit and watch. *Journal of Applied Behavior Analysis*, *23*(3), 353–359. https://doi.org/10.1901/jaba.1990.23-353

Yeager, D. S., Henderson, M. D., Paunesku, D., Walton, G. M., D'Mello, S., Spitzer, B. J., & Duckworth, A. L. (2014). Boring but important: A self-transcendent purpose for learning fosters academic self-regulation. *Journal of Personality and Social Psychology*, *107*(4), 559–580. https://doi.org/10.1037/a0037637

Zins, J. E., Bloodworth, M. R., Weissberg, R. P., & Walberg, H. J. (2004). The scientific base linking social and emotional learning to school success. In J. E. Zins, R. P. Weissberg, M. C. Wang, & H. J. Walberg (Eds.), *Building Academic Success on Social and Emotional Learning* (pp. 3–22). New York: Teachers College Press.

Index

Note: Page numbers in **bold** refer to tables and in *italics* to figures.

24-karat Golden Rule of Education 30

Academy for SEL in Schools 171
ACEs (adverse childhood experiences) 3
achievement 19, 82, 142–143
Adelman, H. S. 19
Adubato, S. 105, *107*
Adult Assessment of Student SDM/SPS Skills 165–166
Allday, R. A. 21
anxiety 38, 69, 82–83, 90, 143
authenticity 22, 94
autonomic arousal 73, 77
Azzam, A. M. 126

Bailey, J. S. 84
Bear, G. 89–90
behavior: expectations 25–27; management 131–134; reflection 135–141; reinforcement 22
Behavioral Reflection Sheet 137–138
Belland, B. R. 123
Benjamin Franklin Middle School, Ridgewood, New Jersey 30
Berkowitz, M. W. 168
Berman, S. 147
BEST communication (Body posture, Eye contact, Saying appropriate things, Tone of voice) 92–98; classroom climate and 27, 30; and conflict de-escalation 134; and disagreement 91; and empathy 60; Joining a New Group 152, *153*, 154; and self-regulation 86
Bhavnagri, N. P. 65
The Big Picture 30, 156–157

Bill of Rights and Responsibilities 30–32
Boorstrom, R. E. 20
Brain Breaks 71–72
brainstorming 48, 63, 127–128, 141, 152, 154
Buber, E. 55
Building Healthy Relationships 99–100
"burnout cascade" 85
Butler, L. 30, 50, 60, 146
Button Pushers 75–77, 80, 139

Cain, J. 49
Cameron, C. 70
CASEL (Collaborative for Academic, Social, and Emotional Learning) 3, 9, 33, 87, 170
"The Cat in the Hat" (Dr Seuss) 49
certificate programs for educators 171–172
character education 83
Character Education Partnership 3, 15
classroom climate 19–32; behavioral expectations 25–27; interactions 22–24; layout 71
classroom constitutions 22, 25, 27, 30–32
cognitive-behavioral perspective 3
cognitive empathy *see* perspective taking
Collaborating States Initiative 170
Collaborative for Academic, Social, and Emotional Learning *see* CASEL
collaborative approach 22, 36, 150
Comer, J. 3
Common Core 6, 117

communication and relationship skills 87–109; defiance 91; educators' 105–109; good 169; I-Messages 101–105; interview preparation 105, 107; positive feedback 91; reflection 91–92; respectful disagreement 91; and teams 108–109
community building 4–5, 20–26, 28–29, 85, 142
competence 10, 15, 36, 143
conflict de-escalation 26, 86, 103, 105–106, 134–135
conflict resolution 89
content 6
context 6–7, 111–112
convergent thinking 126
cooperation 84, 89, 150
courage 16
creativity 126–129; constructive 47, 48
cultural empathy 64–65
curiosity 17
Curriculum Reflection Sheet 159

data, comparative 168
Dealing with Distractions Activity 81–82
depression 143
design thinking 126
developmental networks 4
Dewey, J. 2, 13
Disagreement Box 91
disciplinary situations 25, 26, 90, 97
distractions activity 81–82
distress 57, 148
divergent thinking 126
Dr Seuss 49
Drapeau, P. 126
Dray, A. 35
Duckworth, A. 80

Elias, M. J. 4, 50, 64, 168, 169, 172–173
Elias, M. J. et al. (2014) 3
Elkind, D. 13
emotional hijacking 68, 72–73, 75, 77, 81, 111, 112
Emotional Intelligence (Goleman) 3, 68
emotional regulation skills 27
emotions, verbal and non-verbal expression of 37–41
empathy 54–67; building through literature 63–65; and community 20, 29, 30; creativity and 126;

development of 59–60; and educators 66–67; pedagogies 146–148; social awareness and 33, 35; understanding and 106
empathy awareness breaks 58–59
engagement 12, 24, 65, 90, 91, 114, 142
EQ Quiz for students 162, 166–167
exams, scheduling of 71
expertise, building and sharing 171–172

facilitative questions 115, 116, 119, 121, 124, 133
Facing History and Ourselves initiative 58–59
Fahy, M. 66
feedback: Joining a New Group 152; peer 6, 98; and self-awareness 46; self-regulation 78; skills-oriented approach 11; success and 91, 157–167
Feelings Fingerprints 73–75, 77, 80
Feelings Freeze Frame 40–41
Feelings Jeopardy 38–39
Feelings Memory Match Game 37–38
Feelings role plays with observations 39–40
Feelings Walking Tour 67
FIG Footsteps 60–63, 65, 134
FIG TESPN framework 112–113, 115, 118, 129, 133, 139, 157
fight or flight response 26, 27, 68, 73, 80
Four Corners Game 102, 103–104

Gladwell, M. 11
globalization, and social awareness 60
Glynn, L. 30
Goldilocks zone of stress and achievement 142–143
Goleman, D. 3, 68
Graczyk, P. A. 4
Graesser, A. C. et al. (2018) 114
gratitude 17, 47, 48, 138
Greenberg, M. T. 85
greeting students 21
grit 17, 80
Gross, J. 70
group-oriented instruction 150–151
Gu, J. 123

Hansen, D. T. 20
Harris, A. 89–90

Hendra, M. 59
Hillel 34
historical empathy 65–66
Hoerr, T. R. 57, 67
holistic approach 84
Holmes, V.-L. 144–145, 150
Hudson, MA 147, 148
humanity 16
Hwang, Y. 144–145, 150
Hyman, L. 51

identity 169
Identity and Purpose Interview 42–43
I-messages 89, 91, 101–105
immigration and empathy 64–65
innovation 169
inspiration 28

Jackson, P. W. 20
Jacobson, L. 58, 59
JCAT (The Jewish Court of All
    Time) 65–66
Jennings, P. A. 85
Jigsaw Grouping 114, *115*
John Adams Middle School, Santa
    Monica 58–59
Johnson, D. W. 150, 151
Johnson, R. T. 150, 151
Joining a New Group 151–154
justice 16

Keep Calm 27, 77–80, 83, 84, 139, 141
Kelly, J 22
Kessler, R. 146
Kim, N. J. 123
King, M. L. Jr. 17
KIPP Schools Approach 17–18
Kress, J. 168, 169, 172–173
Kupperman, J. 66

language arts, self- and social awareness
    in 49–53
Language Arts Extension 44
Larson, M. 55
Legacy Goals 26
Liljedahl, P. 114–115
listening, effective 42, 48–49, 57,
    106, 108
Long, D. 7
"The Lorax" (Dr Seuss) 49

Mabry, M. 65
Mantz, L. 89–90
Martin, C. E. 51

Mastering our Skills and Inspiring
    Character *see* MOSAIC
math 82–83, 114, 144, 150
McCarthy, M. H. 147
meaningful work 144–146
meditation 79
Merritt, E. G. 70
mindfulness 3, 77
mirror neurons 54, 55
Missouri 170
mistrust 90
modeling: communication skills
    93–94, 105; conflict de-escalation
    26; effective listening 49; with
    intentional instruction 10–12, 14, 24;
    self-regulation 70
Monobe, G. 64
MOSAIC (Mastering our Skills
    and Inspiring Character) 16–17;
    behavioral expectations 25, 32;
    Behavioral Reflection Sheet 137–138;
    Brain Breaks 72; Identity and Purpose
    Interview Worksheet 42; Planning
    Our Project 121–122; service learning
    and social action 148–149; Three
    Zones Activity 43; virtues 46
motivation 12–13, 141–144;
    communication and 106; empathy
    and 56, 66; and self-regulation 80,
    83, 84; virtues and 16
Mugno, D. 58
myths 169

Naftel, M. 64
National Center for Education and
    Innovation 168
National Schools of Character program
    170–171
neuroimaging 3
neuroscience 3, 34, 54, 55
New Jersey 170
New Jersey School Health and Climate
    Coalition 28
Nigg, J. T. 69
norms: classroom 20, 23, 25–26,
    32, 142; communication and
    90; networks and 4; social
    awareness and 36
Northeast Foundation for Children,
    "Rules for School" 36
Novick, B. 168, 169, 172–173
Novick, B. et al. (2002) 157, 158

optimism 17, 33, 47–48, 143–144

Pahomov, L. 151
Pakurar, K. 21
PAR (practitioner action research) 129
paraphrasing 62, 117
parents, responsibilities of 4–5
peer mediation 79
peer pressure 142
peer relationships 89–90
perseverance 80
perspective taking 33, 35, 45, 56, 60, 66, 134
Peugh, J. L. 70
Physical Education and Sports, self-regulation and 83–84
Pintrich, P. R. 142
Place Out of Time project 65–66
Plato 2
positivity 143–144; and classroom climate 24–25, 27, 28–30; and communication and relationships 89–92, 101, 106; MOSAIC approach 116; peer pressure and 142; and resistance 168, 169; self-awareness and 47–48; self-regulation and 70, 83, 86
poverty 3–4, 88
practitioner action research see PAR
proactive approach: behavior management 25, 132–135; group-oriented instruction 150; pedagogy 6; self-regulation 70, 75, 77, 81
problem solving 9, 167–169; see also SPS (Social Problem Solving)
Problem Solving Zone 133–134
Problem-Solving Framework for Action 158
Promising Practices 170–171

Quilt Project 147

race 3, 148
Ramachandran, V. S. 55
Reaction Tracker 138–139
Reading Feelings Activity 50–51
reflection 13, 15; and behavior 27, 135–141; closure of day and 91–92, 153; collaborative work and 22, 23, 25; constructive 84; educators and 52–53; group work 151; parental 87; reflective self-assessment and 157–159
reflective journals 65, 99–100
resistance 168–169

respect: in classroom 27–28, 30, 32; communication and 90–91, 93, 96–97; empathy and 58; self-regulation and 86; self-respect and 135; social awareness and 33
Responsive Classroom program 21, 36, 90
Rimm-Kaufman, S. E. 70
roadblocks 167
Robinson, K. 125
role models 10, 32
roles, defined 168
Romasz-McDonald, T. 50
Rosenblitt, D. 58
Rozek, C. S. et al. (2019) 82–83
Saarni, C. 59

safety and health 28
scaffolding 143, 145, 148; empathy and 57–59, 65; role plays 12; self-regulation and 70, 75; Social Problem Solving (SPS) and 113, 117–121, 123, 124, 128
scheduling 70–71, 144
Schmid, P. F. 55
School Development Project 3
SEL (Social and Emotional Learning) 7; and academics 146–150; communication and 88; early programs 34; empathy and 29, 59; group-oriented instruction 151; motivation to develop skills 12–13; order of 88; skills-oriented approach 14–16
SEL4US 171
self-awareness 4, 9, 33–37, 41–48, 49–53, 151
self-control 17, 27, 68–69, 70, 84, 165
self-determination theory 143
self-monitoring 11, 108, 135–136
self-oriented purpose 144
self-reflection 52–53, 135, 151
self-regulation 9, 68–86; Brain Breaks 71–72; Button Pushers 75–76; Dealing with Distractions Activity 81–82; for educators 85–86; empathy and 57; Feelings Fingerprints 73–74; Keep Calm 77–80; in math 82–83; and modeling 70; physical education and sports 83–84; proactive approach 70; STEM 82–83
self-respect 135
self-transcendent purpose 144
self-understanding 34, 46

Selman, R. 12, 35
service learning and social action 146–147
Service Learning-Social Action Planning Worksheet 148, 149
Shady, S. L. H. 55
Sharing Circles 15, 23–24, 37, 44, 70, 76
Sigel, I. 13, 56
Signature Strengths Approach 16
situation selection 70
situational modification 70
Sizer, N. F. 20
Sizer, T. 20
Skills Practice Worksheet 135, 136
skills-oriented approach 8–18; complex skills 12; component skills development 10; feedback 11–12; intentionality 10–12; modeling 10–12, 14; motivation 12–13, 14; naming 13; pedagogy for generalizing skills 14–15; reflection 13, 15; reinforcement 15; Signature Strengths Approach 16
Social and Emotional Learning *see* SEL
social awareness 9, 33–53; for educators 51–53; effective listening 48–49; in language arts 49–51; verbal expression 37–48
Social Decision Making 27, 72, 159–165
social intelligence 17–18
social media 45, 88
SPS (Social Problem Solving) 110–129; for educators 129; emotions and 111; and environmental problems 123–125; facilitative questioning 115–116; FIG TESPN Framework 112–113; group work and 114–115; Jigsaw Grouping 114, *115*; and project planning 121–123; questioning strategies 116–117; Scaffolding Worksheet 118–121; and science 123–125; Visual Arts 128–129
socioscience 123
Son, E. H. 64
Stanzler, J. 66
STEM, self-regulation and 82–83
Stern, R. 51
STOP Procedure 140–141
stress 26–27, 72, 79, 80, 82–86, 142–143

Student Study Skills Improvement Plan 145–146
supportive environment 3, 19, 28, 142, 169
sustainability **167**

Tarfon, Rabbi 129
Taylor, L. 19
teacher language 58
teacher turnover 3–4
temperance 16
Three Zone "Yes-No-Maybe" Discussions 43–45, 67
Tierney, W. G. 168
time frames, agreed 168
Time Out 83, 133
transcendence 16
transition to learning 21–22, 70
transition rituals 23
Trigger Situation Monitor 52
triggers 71, 70
Trouble Tracker 138, 140
trust 142
Turner, D. J. 123
Two Question Rule 117, 128

UCLA, National Center for History in the Schools' Historical Thinking Standards 6

Vande Zande, R. et al. (2014) 128
virtues 2, 15–18, 46–48, 135–136, 138
Virtues Monitor 135, 136
Vision and Mission Statements 156–157
Visual Arts 128–129
visualization 67
Vygotsky, L., Zone of Proximal Development 143

Wanless, S. B. 70
"The Way I Feel" ("Así me siento yo") (Cain) 49
White, A. G. 84
whole child education 28
wisdom 16

Yeager, D. S. et al. (2014) 144
Yerkes-Dodson principle 12

zest 17
Zins, J. E. 4
Zins, J. E. et al. (2004) 7